GROLIER'S
AMAZING WORLD OF ANIMALS

GROLIER ENTERPRISES INC.

Editor – HERBERT KONDO

Grolier Enterprises Inc.

Publisher – ROBERT B. CLARKE

Library of Congress Catalog Card Number 71-141898
© 1970, 1971, 1972 Fratelli Fabbri Editori, Milan
Text: © 1972 Grolier Enterprises, Inc.
Illustrations*: © 1968, 1971, 1972 Fratelli Fabbri Editori, Milan

Cover and Title Page Design: KIRCHOFF/WOHLBERG, INC.

Cover Photo Credit: Photo Researchers, Inc., Thomas Martin.

Title Page Photo Credit: Photo Researchers, Inc., Susan McCartney.

Photo Credits:

Animals, Animals—43, 71, 89, 112; Atlas–Merlet—90, Vienne—107; Barnaby's Picture Library—55, 56, 70, 78, 124, 128, 137; Alan Cash—51; Bruce Coleman Ltd. Des
Bartlett—75, 117, Bob Campbell—81, Sven Gillsatler—70, James Hyatt—86, Peter Jackson—100, 102, 103, Russ Kinne—19, 76, 77, 112, P. Myers—11, R. T.
Peterson—109, James Simon—104; Comet—46; Otto Diehl—133; E. Dulevant—107; E.P.S.—26, 33, 38, 40; Framarin—42; Dr. S. Frugis—79; Lucio Gaggero—31, 93;
Helmut Heimpeo—54; Ingmar Holmasen—79, 83, 85, 92, 98, 106, 107, 108, 112, 113, 127, 140; E. Hosking—16, 73, 75, 131; C. Lederer—31, 67; Leidmann—56, 57; Loke Wan
Tho—105; Longo—27, 31, 116; Marconato–A.S.C.P.—41; A. Margiocco—23; G. Mazza—58; Melde—128; Museum of Natural History—Milan—13, 65; National Historical
Photographic Agency—A. M. Anderson—127, F. Blackburn—128, J. B. Blossom—136, D. N. Dalton—114, 141, P. Wayre—132; C. Ostman—31; C. Ott—73; A. Pazzuconi
—133; Dr. L. Pellegrini—50, 51; Willis Peterson—129; Photo Trends—7; Picturepoint—75, 138, 139; N. Plosser—71; Paul Popper—25, 31, 57, 58, 60, 68, 69, 77, 79, 87, 89,
91, 99, 113, 137; Roebild-Muller—7, 18, 20; Edward Rosenberg—28, 35, 41, 84; A. P. Rossi—30, 47, 70, 71, 82, 85, 96, 99, 101, 104, 105, 114, 115, 119, 122, 130, 133, 135;
Schunemann—32, 34; Schuster—19; S.E.F.—62, 66, 69; Sirman–Dimt—83; A. Thau—110, 134, 135; Tierbilder–Okapia—28, 29, 44, 55, 57, 66, 68, 71, 118, 119, 126; Tom-
isch—108; G. Vecchia—84, 85, 124, 125; V. Dia—14, 16, 51; World Wildlife Fund—26, 32; ZFA—17, 22, 24, 60, 105.

*Photographs other than those listed above are credited to Fratelli Fabbri Editori.

CONTENTS

LIVING BIRDS

Living Birds

In this volume, we continue our discussion of the members of the class Aves. We will look at some of the best-known and most colorful species—birds such as chickens and pheasants, gulls and sandpipers, pigeons and owls, hummingbirds and parrots, and the exotic peacocks, lyrebirds, and birds-of-paradise. Some of these creatures are almost worldwide in distribution, while others are found in very limited, often remote, areas.

Chickens and Their Relatives—Galliformes

The order Galliformes is one of the two important groups of game birds. This order, with 7 families and more than 250 species, includes such diverse birds as the exotic peacock, the domestic chicken, and the widely hunted pheasant. Galliformes can be found in both the Old and New Worlds.

Most species live on or near the ground. They have strong, usually spurred, legs that are well-adapted for running and walking. Each foot has three toes in front and one behind, usually in a slightly raised position. These toes make excellent scratching tools for uncovering the seeds, grains, and fruits that are the general diet of these birds.

The Galliformes often have elaborate tails with 8 to 32 quill feathers. The plumage, which is soft and abundant, is generally more brilliant in the male than it is in the female. Many are polygamous. The hen's eggs are generally laid in a very simple nest, consisting of a slight depression in the ground.

The Family Megapodiidae includes scrubfowl, junglefowl, mallee fowl, and brush turkeys. There are seven genera in this family; they are found only in Australia, New Guinea, and a few surrounding islands.

Megapodes are fairly large birds with dull plumage, usually brown or blackish. The tail is long, and the head is frequently featherless. The males of this family build the nest, which consists of a large mound of debris. The eggs are incubated in the mound by heat from the sun or from decaying materials, rather than by the body heat of the adult bird. These mounds are impressive, sometimes reaching heights of 20 feet and widths of 50 feet, although the builder is often not more than 28 inches long.

The Scrubfowl, *Megapodius freycinet*, builds mounds of dead leaves, which decay to provide the incubating heat. These birds seem to have an instinct for providing just the right amount of heat, since the proportions of organic and inorganic matter are carefully determined by the position of the mound and the humidity of the atmosphere.

Junglefowl of the genera *Megacephalon*, *Eulipoa*, and *Megapodius* lay their eggs in a hole dug in the sand and exposed to the sun. The hole is later covered, and the heat reaches the egg through the surface soil. Careful selection of the site provides just the proper temperature. In some regions, such as the Solomon Islands, the eggs are laid in holes dug in ground that is warmed by volcanic steam.

The Mallee Fowl, *Leipoa ocellata*, lives in the sparse arid bushland of Australia. There, the air temperature undergoes daily and seasonal fluctuations that have a corresponding effect on the temperature of the earth. Hence, the mallee fowl faces a more complex heat-control problem than the other megapodes when it comes to incubating the eggs.

They dig a hole about 9 feet wide and 3 feet deep. During the southern winter, the birds gather vegetation from the surrounding area and fill in the hole. After the sea-

The black curassow (opposite page), with its characteristic crest of curly feathers, is a member of the family Cracidae. These fowllike birds inhabit forests and feed on fruit and tender leaves. The male utters a very low-pitched "droning" song.

sonal rains have dampened the vegetation, the birds cover it with a 2-foot layer of sand that isolates the wet vegetation and encourages its decay. The ideal temperature for the egg chamber is 92°F. The temperature is controlled by the male bird, who spends about five hours daily regulating it. If the temperature in the chamber is too high, the bird opens the incubation area in the cool morning hours. If it is too cold, he exposes it to the warm rays of the sun.

The male is apparently jealous of his responsibility and allows the female to approach the mound only to lay her eggs. Since the eggs are laid over a long period of time, they hatch separately.

Once an egg is ready to hatch, its parents seem to lose interest, and the chick is left to pick its way through the shell and upwards through the sand. Independent from birth, the chick is ready to fly less than 15 hours after it is born, and it flutters up into bushes to roost.

Brush Turkeys of the genera *Aepypodius*, *Alectura*, and *Talegalla* live in dense tropical forests or brushlands. The male prepares the nesting mounds, which are about 3 feet high and 3½ feet in diameter. He controls the temperature by stirring the decaying vegetable matter with his bill, which serves him as a sort of natural thermometer.

Curassows, Chachalacas, and Guans of the family Cracidae are all residents of tropical and subtropical regions of the New World. This family includes 11 genera with about 40 species. They are slender birds with long tails, elegant head plumage, and considerable vocal talents.

Some species can produce a variety of noises, from raucous cries to whistles and lamentlike sounds. Because of the presence of an extended windpipe, which sometimes reaches the abdomen, and a system of air chambers in the neck, the calls of these birds resound loudly and clearly.

The brush turkey has a featherless head and a long tail. With its large, strong feet, it constructs a pit, then lays eggs inside. The bird protects the eggs with a covering of earth and vegetation.

The Cracidae may be as small as a large partridge or as large as a slender wild turkey. The bill is strong and curved, and the wings are short and rounded. These birds pick up their food directly with their bills instead of first scratching for it with their toes. They also gather fruit or tender shoots from trees.

Members of this family are monogamous. They are the only fowl-like birds that regularly nest in trees. Individual nests, small and crude, are built in the lower branches of a tree, often over water. There are generally two to four eggs in a clutch, and incubation lasts from 22 to 34 days. The young are born with such well-developed wings that they leave the nest very quickly and learn to fly within their first week.

The curassows of the genera *Crax*, *Mitu*, and *Pauxi* are characterized by a prominent black crest with metallic highlights. They prefer to live in trees and show considerable agility in moving from branch to branch because of their powerful gripping toes—a characteristic that sets them apart from other gallinaceous birds.

The great, or Mexican, curassow, *Crax rubra*, is one of the largest of the Cracidae. It may weigh as much as 10 pounds. Males are black with green highlights. They have elegant crests, and there is a large yellow knob at the base of the beak.

The guans include about 12 species, mostly of the genus *Penelope*. Males and females have much the same coloring—chiefly brown and olive.

The chachalacas include 11 species of the genus *Ortalis*. For the most part, they are brown and olive in color; their throat is without feathers and brick-red in color. One species is found in southern Texas, but the other chachalacas live farther south.

The Grouse Family, Tetraonidae, includes ptarmigans, capercaillies, prairie chickens, and heath hens, as well as other types of grouse. These birds have feet that act like

The razor-billed curassow (below left) builds a small, crude nest of clumsily-joined twigs. Unlike most fowl, it lays only two eggs at a time.

A mallee fowl (below), one of the megapodes, or "incubator birds," is shown here at its nest mound. The male digs the mound open each time the female comes to deposit an egg.

efficient snowshoes. They are well-known for their elaborate courting dances. The members of this family vary greatly in the degree of color differences between the sexes.

Adapted to cold climates, most Tetraonidae have a row of teethlike projections on their toes that keeps them from sinking into the snow. The ptarmigans have a layer of stiff feathers that perform a similar function—an important adaptation to their habitats, which range from the tundras of North America to arctic and sub-arctic regions, and from the Alps and Pyrenees to northern England and Scotland.

In order to camouflage themselves, some Tetraonidae have developed a sophisticated method of protection. Their plumage changes from brown and black to white, according to the season. Molting three times a year permits them to fade into the ever-changing landscape. Other species in lands with little snowfall have not developed the protective white winter coloring and remain dark all year.

The spruce grouse (right) lives in the evergreen forests of North America, especially those of Canada and Alaska. Displaying males, like this one, have an inflated patch of red skin over each eye.

The overall physical characteristics of the Tetraonidae are basically the same. The bill is short and strong—although the capercaillie has a somewhat hooked, aquiline bill. Some of the ptarmigans, as well as other grouse, have inflatable areas of skin over the eyes. These areas are generally red. The birds vary from 12 inches to 3 feet in length, and weigh as much as 16 pounds. The hind toe is slightly elevated, and the shank of the leg is usually quite feathered. Otherwise, grouse closely resemble pheasants. Taxonomists sometimes group these birds together.

Both Eurasian and North American grouse are known for their mating rituals. During the breeding season the lesser prairie chickens, *Tympanuchus pallidicinctus*, of the North American dry plains, gather on communal dancing grounds, where the males strut, inflate reddish neck sacs, erect horn-like neck feathers, and produce a series of booming sounds. In North America the ruffed grouse, *Bonasa umbellus*, fans the air with its wings to attract attention; in Eurasia the black grouse, *Lyrurus tetrix*, divide their dancing grounds into individual territories, which each male defends ferociously before courting any female that happens to come to visit him.

Among the capercaillies, *Tetrao urogallus*, and black grouse, the males and females have decidedly different appearances; the males are larger and equipped with flamboyant red or orange wattles. Males of the North American genera *Dendragapus* and *Tympanuchus* have inflatable air sacs. Bare orange, red, or violet skin on the neck gives the males of these two species a grotesque appearance, especially when he swells out his neck and spreads his tail feathers. This display occurs only when several males get together on their mating grounds. Solitary displays are typical only of species inhabiting forests and of ptarmigans.

The nest is a simple depression in the ground, often at the base of a large tree.

The clutch varies from 6 to 12 eggs, depending on the species, and is incubated by the hen alone. These birds are mainly herbivorous. The black grouse, for example, eats whortle-berries and rhododendron buds, while in winter the capercaillie consumes great quantities of pine-tree needles.

Species living in the mountains move down to lower altitudes in winter to take advantage of the smaller snowfalls. Mountain forest grouse include the hazel hen, or hazel grouse, *Tetrastes bonasia*. The white-tailed ptarmigan, *Lagopus leucurus*, inhabits the frozen treeless mountain tundra of North America. Willow and rock ptarmigans, *L. lagopus* and *L. mutus*, live in arctic and sub-arctic regions. Ptarmigans can also be found in the Alps and Pyrenees.

Pine forests are the habitat of the capercaillie and the Siberian capercaillie, *Tetrao pavirostris*. The black grouse and its cousin, the Eurasian black grouse, *Lyrurus mlokosiewiczi*, are residents of Eurasia. The lesser prairie chicken and the greater prairie chicken, *Tympanuchus cupido*, prefer open ground, especially the great prairies.

Pheasants, Partridges, Peacocks, and Quails are members of the family Phasianidae. The Phasianidae are more varied and more populous than other Galliformes. Some of them, particularly some of the pheasants, are among the most beautiful birds in the world. One of the phasianids, the red junglefowl, *Gallus gallus,* is the ancestor of the barnyard chicken; this bird has been domesticated since about 4,000 B.C.

The phasianids are chiefly Old World species. They are represented in the New World only by the American quail of the sub-family Odontophorinae. Turkeys and grouse are sometimes placed in this family.

Americans tend to confuse grouse, partridges, and quails. This confusion was probably caused by early settlers who named the New World birds according to their resem-

The cock sage grouse of western North America is shown here in its strutting display pose. Several males gather on a dancing ground, or "lek," to compete for mates.

blance to the birds of the settler's homelands.

In spite of their worldwide distribution and the variations in size, shape, and color, members of the family Phasianidae share many characteristics. Most nest on the ground, although in some species, the birds roost in trees at night. Males are equipped with up to three spurs on each leg. They all forage for food by scratching the ground with their feet. Their stout legs and powerful toes and nails are well-adapted for digging up roots, bulbs, insects, larvae, and worms; their short, thick bills are excellent for picking berries and seeds, their main diet.

Except for a few species of migratory quail, the Phasianidae are sedentary. Their short, rounded wings are capable of spurts of powerful flight, but these birds cannot remain in flight for any sustained period. The nest is always simple, and usually placed on the ground. The hen incubates the eggs, but the rearing of the young is often shared by both parents.

One of the most remarkable characteristics of the Phasianidae is the tail, which ranges from the short tail of certain quail to the long and elaborate appendage of pheasants. The spectacular tail plumage is displayed by the males in the mating season to attract females.

Reeves Pheasant, *Syrmaticus reevesi,* has one of the most impressive tails in the family Phasianidae. Its brilliant plumage ranges from golden yellow to copper red to dark blue, with spots and stripes of gray, black,

The chukar, or rock partridge, lives in dry areas from the Middle East to northern India. Thousands of chukars have been introduced into the United States, and they have become established as gamebirds in the Southwest.

and white. These birds live in mountainous areas from Burma to China and from Formosa to Japan.

The Crested Argus, *Rheinartia ocellata,* has the largest tail feathers of any bird. Measuring at least 5 feet, the tail of this bird is brown with a delicate design of buff and black spots. The crested argus is native to Indochina, and may be extinct as the result of the war.

New World Quails of the subfamily Odontophorinae include 36 species. These birds are a little larger than their Old World relatives. The American species have stouter beaks, which are sharply pointed and have sawtoothed edges.

New World quail are found from the temperate zone of North America to southern Brazil. Various species are found in forests, particularly tropical forests, while others prefer bush or desert terrain.

The bobwhite, *Colinus virginianus,* is one of the best-known American quails and one of the most popular game birds in the

United States. It is found from southern Canada to Guatemala. Closely related species live in Central America, Colombia, and Venezuela, and efforts have been made to introduce the bobwhite to Europe.

The California quail, *Lophortyx californica,* is a well-known species in this subfamily. It is found in the southwestern United States. The scaled quail, *Callipepla squamata,* is noted for its beauty. Also known as the cottontop because of its white crest, it, too, lives in the southwestern United States.

Old World Quail belong to the genus *Coturnix.* They are smaller than their American cousins—some are no bigger than sparrows. The common quail of Eurasia, *Coturnix coturnix,* is the most widely distributed species. It is migratory, but sedentary "cousins" can be found in Africa, India, and New Zealand.

Two very small species are the painted quail, which has blue coloring on its breast and stomach, and the swamp, or brown, quail, of Australia and New Guinea. They are sometimes placed in their own genera, *Excalfactoria* and *Synoicus,* respectively.

The lively roulroul, one of the Asiatic partridges (above left), lives in Malaysia. Its crest is bright crimson. Its body colors are red, blue, and green.

The California quail (above right) is one species of American quail. Where not hunted, these birds become tame, and small flocks often walk through shrubbery and gardens.

Partridges. The birds that are called partridges in Europe are simply large quails. Partridges have longer tails, stronger bills and legs, and a more contrasted coloring than the smaller quail species. Like the quail, partridges are popular game birds.

The gray partridge, *Perdix perdix,* is hunted on the plains and farmlands of Europe. It has been introduced in North America under the name Hungarian partridge. A closely related species, *P. arbata,* inhabits the fields of Asia from Turkestan to China. *P. hodgsoniae* lives high in the Himalayas and has a curious horseshoe marking on its belly that sets it apart.

The red-legged partridge, *Alectoris rufa,* is found from southern France to the Canary Islands. A related species, *A. barbara,* inhabits Sardinia and North Africa. The chukar, *A. graeca,* is rather widely distributed in the Alps and Apennines and in part of southeastern Europe. Members of these three species have red bills and legs. There are striking black bars on the flanks variously edged with gray, chestnut, and brown. In some, a more or less well-defined black collar extends from the space between the eyes and the bill to the sides of the neck and down to the chest.

The tree partridges belong to the genus *Arborophila.* They have soft plumage, a short bill and tail, and long spurless legs. They are variously colored. Tree partridges are native to the forests of southern China, India, and Malaysia.

Malaysia, Borneo, and Sumatra are inhabited by the black wood partridge, *Melanoperdix nigra,* the crimson-headed partridges of the genus *Haematortyx,* and the curious roulroul, *Rollulus roulroul,* which has a blue, green, and red coloring and a beautiful scarlet crest. The bamboo partridges of the genus

The male pheasant (below left) is strikingly colorful. Introduced into England by the Romans, the ring-necked pheasant is now also common in much of the United States.

A female ring-necked pheasant (below right) blends easily into the grass and brush around it.

Bambusicola are small partridges found in China and Indochina.

Snowcocks, which are about the same size as pheasants, are found in mountainous areas from the Caucasus to Mongolia. They are classified in three genera—*Tetraogallus, Tetraophasis,* and *Lerwa.*

Spurfowl comprise three species in the genus *Galloperdix.* These birds look like small pheasants, with an area of bare skin around the eyes. The long legs have three or four spurs in the male and one or two in the female. Spurfowls inhabit India and Ceylon.

The Francolins of the genus *Francolinus* include 5 Asian and 36 African species. *F. francolinus* is found as far north as the Mediterranean. The general coloring is a protective brown with various spots and streaks, although black, white, and chestnut predominate in some species. There are spurs on the legs. In size the francolins range from the dimensions of a partridge to those of a pheasant hen.

The True Pheasants of the subfamily Phasianinae include 16 genera and 49 species. The most striking characteristic of these birds is their beautiful, elaborate plumage, especially the male's.

The blood pheasant, *Ithaginis cruentus,* is rather small and similar to a partridge in shape. The male has lacy plumage in various shades of gray, light green, and crimson; there are also black markings. There are several spurs on the red legs. Blood pheasants live high in the Himalayas.

Tragopans, unlike other Phasianidae, spend much time in trees. They often lay their eggs in old nests of crows or other birds. They are found in thick forests at high altitudes in central and southern Asia.

Males of the five *Tragopan* species have a rather short, laterally compressed tail.

They are variously spotted with white against a red, ochre, or gray coloring, depending on the species. The face and throat are featherless, and the skin is brilliantly colored in blue, orange, or yellow. The head has two erect blue "horns" of flesh; the skin beneath the bill can be distended in courtship to form a huge "bib." The hens are much more soberly colored; they are brown with lighter and darker spots and bars.

The koklass, *Pucrasia macrolopha,* is found in the Himalayas and the mountainous regions of nearby China, but their preferred habitat is more open country. The male has a large double crest, a pointed tail and "lanceolate" plumage, which is light colored with brown, gray, chestnut, or black streaks.

The Impeyan pheasant, *Lophophorus impejanus,* is found in the same areas as the koklass. A large bird with a short, squared-off tail, the cock of this species has a fairly well-developed crest. He is splendidly colored with metallic green, blue, purple, and copper above and a velvety black on the under-

The "ears" of the eared pheasant are only tufts of white feathers. This is one of the few species of pheasant in which the males and females have identical plumage. Eared pheasants were once common around monasteries in Tibet.

The argus pheasant (top) has a brilliant, 4-foot-long ocellated, or "eyed," tail. It lives in the thick jungles of Southeast Asia.

The common peafowl (center) is often called a peacock. This refers only to males, however; females are peahens. The brilliant coloration comes from the refraction and reflection of light from layers of feathers.

The Lady Amherst's pheasant (bottom) lives in the mountains of central-western China.

parts. The hens, which are smaller, are brown streaked with black.

Gallopheasants are found mostly at moderate altitudes from the Himalayan mountain forests east to China and Malaysia. These birds include ten species of the genus *Lophura*. All have a long, arched tail, black plumage on the underparts, and combinations of black, blue, violet, and white above. There are various types of crests or "ears" on the head, and velvety red and blue wattles adorn the face. The legs are bright red.

The eared pheasants of the genus *Crossoptilon* have prominent, white-feathered "ears." They are the only true pheasants in which the male is not more brilliantly colored than the female. The eared pheasants resemble gallopheasants except that the plumage is less compact, especially on the tail, where the feathers are hairlike and reminiscent of egret plumes. There are three species native to the valleys of Tibet and northwest China.

The cheer, *Catreus wallichi*, has a crest and a long tail. In the males the plumage is gray spotted with black and tempered to reddish on the wings and rump.

The green pheasant, *Phasianus versicolor*, is found in Japan, while the ring-necked pheasant, *P. colchicus*, is found in Asia from the Caucasus to the China Sea. There are a large number of subspecies of ring-necked pheasant, many with characteristic and colorful names. They have been introduced very successfully into North America, Europe, New Zealand, and other regions.

The golden pheasant, *Chrysolophus pictus*, and the Lady Amherst's pheasant, *C. amherstiae*, are two splendid smaller pheasants from the mountains of central Asia. The head of the male is adorned with a long, curved crest. The nape and neck are covered by an abundant ruff of broad feathers; the ruff is yellow on the golden pheasant and white on the Lady Amherst. The rest of the plumage of both birds is a mixture of yellow, red, green, blue, and white.

The peacock pheasants of the genus *Polyplectron* are small pheasants with a long, graduated tail. They have gray or brown plumage adorned by green or metallic violet "eyes." Peacock pheasants live in the thick tropical forests of southest Asia from India to the Indonesian island of Borneo.

The great argus, *Argusianus argus*, has bare bluish skin on the head and neck. The two extremely long central tail feathers are gray and brown with white spots. The body plumage is variously spotted with chestnut, yellow, and black; the enormous secondary feathers are broadened at the tips and adorned with longitudinal rows of green nonmetallic "eyes." The great argus is found in Malaysia, Sumatra, and Borneo.

The male golden pheasant (left) is one of the most colorful of the pheasants of Asia. Originally found in China, it has been introduced in Europe. The golden pheasant is a familiar subject for artists and poets of the Far East.

Peafowl of the genus *Pavo* are commonly known as peacocks. The blue peafowl, *P. cristatus*, has been raised in captivity for at least 20 centuries, with little change except for variations in coloring. These birds are native to India and Ceylon. The green peafowl, *P. muticus*, is found from Burma to Java.

The Congo peacock, *Afropavo congensis*, caused a considerable sensation among zoologists when it was discovered in 1937. It was found in the Congo rain forests by the ornithologist James Chapin—until that time no true pheasants had been found in Africa. The handsome male has a curious white and black double crest and green and blue plumage. The continued existence of these birds is being menaced by man's destruction of the African rain forests.

Turkeys are members of the family Meleagrididae. These birds were originally found only in North America, but they have been spread by man to the rest of the world.

Turkeys were named by the first settlers in the New World, who confused these fowl of the family Meleagrididae with the turkey cock (helmeted guineafowl) of the Old World. The wild turkey had been domesticated by the Aztec Indians long before the arrival of the first European settlers.

But in the United States the turkey has come to be thoroughly associated with the Pilgrim Fathers and, of course, the special

holiday of Thanksgiving. Benjamin Franklin even wanted the turkey to replace the bald eagle as the national emblem.

The wild turkey, *Meleagris gallopavo*, is the ancestor of the domestic turkey. Smaller than its domestic brother, the wild turkey may weigh up to 20 pounds. Its feathers are dark, with metallic reflections of bright green, coppery red, and bronze. The wattles on the head, neck, and throat vary in color from red to blue to white. The skin of the neck and head is featherless and reddens in the springtime. In courtship, the male fans out his tail and makes a puffing sound accompanied by the famous "gobble."

The wild turkey has strong legs, and it runs well. However, it can make only short

The vulturine guineafowl (top) and the crested guineafowl (below) are two cousins of the guineafowl on the opposite page.

The wild turkey (left), ancestor of the larger domestic turkey, may weigh as much as 20 pounds.

The Guineafowl of the family Numididae all inhabit Africa and the neighboring island of Madagascar. The four genera consist of medium-size birds that prefer termites to other foods. However, they eat a wide variety of vegetable and animal matter. Each genus has its own type of headgear.

The helmeted guineafowl, *Numida meleagris,* has a helmet composed of bone. The plumage varies, but the back is always gray, and there is dark gray on the underparts. There are also varying numbers of randomly arranged white spots. Subspecies are found in Africa south of the Sahara, as well as on the islands of Zanzibar and Madagascar.

The helmeted guineafowl is the ancestor of the domestic guineafowl, which is still raised in many parts of the world, although it is less prolific than the domestic chicken.

The crested guineafowl, *Guttera edouardi,* is closely related to the helmeted guineafowl. It has a tuft of curly black feathers on its head. The plumed guineafowl, *G. plumifera,* has a tuft of stiff erect bristles on its head. The Kenya crested guineafowl, *G. pucherani,* has a distinctive and effective coloring; the head and neck are a beautiful cobalt blue, while the throat and the area around the eyes are a bright red. The basic coloring of these birds is closer to black than to gray, with small white spots and a pale blue border. This species prefer dense vegetation, even forest land, to fields and plains.

The white-breasted guineafowl, *Agelastes meleagrides,* is a rare bird that is found only in Ghana and Liberia. It has a bright red head; the breast and mantle are white, and the rest of its body is black.

The smallest member of this genus is the black guineafowl, *Agelastes niger,* which lives only in Guinea. It has a red head and neck decorated by a short stiff mane of black feathers. The rest of its plumage is coal black.

The vulturine guineafowl, *Acryllium vulturinum,* is the most curious member of the

The wattled crane (above) is one of the less handsome members of its family. But all cranes are impressive in flight.

sustained flights. It is one of the wariest of game birds, and its pursuit requires great skill. Good conservation practices are bringing this bird back to some areas.

The ocellated turkey, *Agriocharis ocellata,* is the only other species in the meleagridid family. It gets its name from the *ocelli,* or eyelike spots, on its tail feathers. Once abundant from the Yucatan to Guatemala, it is now seldom seen.

family Numididae. The lone representative of its genus, its featherless head and neck are gray-blue. There is an unusual horseshoe-shaped adornment of chestnut-colored downy feathers at the nape. The body plumage is black on top and cobalt blue on the underparts. At its neck is a necklace of black feathers with white shafts edged in blue. The vulturine guineafowl has crimson-colored eyes.

The Hoatzin, *Opisthocomus hoazin,* is the sole representative of the family Opisthocomidae. It is a tropical bird that lives in the branches of trees, where it flies awkwardly from branch to branch or from tree to tree.

The hoatzin hatches from its egg equipped with rudimentary claws on its wings. This wing structure is somewhat similar to that of the earliest-known bird, *Archaeopteryx*. This remarkable set of claws gives the baby hoatzin a curious four-footed appearance. Indeed, the 19th-century naturalist who was probably the first to study *Opisthocomus* declared, "From an egg laid by a two-footed, two-winged bird hatches a quadruped animal." The claws drop off during the bird's infancy, and the adult has normal wings.

A few hours after birth, the hoatzin chick can leave its nest, which is usually near a river, and move about in the bushes. If frightened, it drops into the water, then later climbs back—using its foreclaws as well as its feet—among the twigs that line the river banks.

The hoatzin has a second characteristic that sets it apart from all other birds. This is its huge crop. This enormous pouch, which serves as a storage receptacle for food, takes up most of the upper third of the bird's body. This means that its chest has special anatomical modifications that are not found in other known bird species. It is supposed that the hoatzin stores its favorite food—tender vegetation—in the crop.

Marsh Birds—Gruiformes

Members of the order Gruiformes are commonly known as marsh birds. They fly poorly. Nonetheless, some migrate long distances, and they have managed to colonize remote oceanic islands. They are well-adapted to ground-living, but they are even better equipped to make their way in lakes,

This exotic bird is the hoatzin, the only living member of the family Opisthocomidae. Here we see only the head with its curious crest. Usually classified with the fowls, it may be a specialized cuckoo.

rivers, and marshes. The Gruiformes are an ancient order; some of the families have only one or two living species.

The order includes many families that seem to have little in common. However, sufficient anatomical and structural similarities exist to merit placing them within the Gruiformes. Some naturalists prefer to classify these marsh birds in other orders. In fact, the Stresemann system of classification treats the eight suborders as separate, individual orders.

Gruiformes are divided into 12 families. Only 3 families, however, have a fair number of species—the Gruidae, Rallidae, and Otididae. Four families have only a single species.

The Roatelos, or Mesites, are members of the family Mesitornithidae. In general, these birds look like thrush-sized rails and walk like pigeons. In fact, they seem to prefer walking or running to flying, even when threatened. Some naturalists assert that roatelos are unable to fly. Even their nests, which consist of a platform of twigs lined with grass and leaves, are placed close to the ground, and they can be reached by hopping rather than flying.

Little is known about the nesting habits of these birds. Apparently a single white glossy egg is laid and, when hatched, the chick is covered with down. In at least one species, the males build the nests and incubate the eggs.

Roatelos have a long tail, short, rounded wings, and well-developed feet. The bill is always slender, and is either short and straight or long and curved. Their coloring runs to a soft brown with white underparts. These birds have five patches of down, similar to those seen on herons.

The three species of the roatelo family, *Mesitornis unicolor, Mesitornis variegata,* and *Monis benschi,* are found only on Madagascar. The two species of the genus *Mesitornis*

The African crowned crane (opposite page) is common in the wild, and does well in captivity also. The crest feathers are bristlelike.

live, respectively, in tropical and dry forests of the island. *Monis benschi* is found only in the vast brushlands of the southern area. All three feed on seeds and insects.

The Buttonquails make up the family Turnicidae. In these birds the roles of the males and females are reversed. The female has the brilliant plumage generally seen in males; the duller-colored males takes care of the incubation of the clutch, as well as the fledglings. The female, however, contributes an equal share in the task of building the family nest. The clutch of eggs averages four, and the incubation period lasts only 13 days. The young mature rapidly and soon become independent.

These birds, like many others, have different plumages at various stages of their development. For example, the down of the newly hatched bird soon becomes the plumage of the juvenile, which in time becomes the adult plumage, and then almost immediately changes into the courting plumage.

Buttonquail have certain habits and physical characteristics similar to those of the true quail, such as a retiring nature and the structure of the bill. A distinguishing feature is the presence of only three front toes and no hind toe.

The family Turnicidae includes 15 species. All are limited to the Old World and prefer warm climates. These birds live in both dry and swampy areas of low-growing brush. They rarely venture into open woodland. They feed on a combination of seeds, insects, and shoots. Like pigeons, they drink continuously without lifting their heads after each swallow. Although they are capable flyers, these birds rarely take to the wing. Some species, however, do migrate and others are wanderers.

Of the 15 species, only the larkquail, *Ortyxelos meiffrenil,* lives in the sandy scrub of central Africa. The others are found throughout Africa and the warmer parts of

Asia, Australia, and Madagascar. One species, variously called the buttonquail, or Andalusian hemipode, *Turnix sylvatica,* inhabits southern Spain. The barred, or common, bustardquail, *T. suscitator,* is found from India to southeast Asia. The female has a splendid nuptial plumage of black feathers around the throat and chest, and is one of the handsomest females in the bird world, where females are often rather dowdy.

The plains-wanderer, or collared hemipode, *Pedionomus torquatus,* is a small bird similar to the buttonquail. However, it is distinguished by the presence of a hind toe, paired carotid arteries, pear-shaped (rather than oval) eggs, and a less suspicious manner. Sometimes, instead of being classified with the buttonquail, this bird is placed in its own family, Pedionomidae.

The plains-wanderer also resembles the bustards by walking with the neck distended in an erect position. In this species, as in the buttonquail, the male has more modest plumage than the female and is in charge of the incubation of the eggs and the rearing of the young.

A rare bird, the plains-wanderer is found only in certain open areas of Australia. There seems to be no current danger of extinction, but this species is being reduced in number as a result of the gradual but relentless destruction of its habitat.

The Cranes belong to the family Gruidae. They are large birds, with long legs and necks. They like to wade in marshy waters. Cranes resemble storks and herons, but their toes are shorter, and their bills shorter with blunted beaks. They have an aristocratic appearance and elegant plumage, which varies from white to slate, with black quill feathers on the wings.

Except for two species, cranes shed all their flight feathers simultaneously and are grounded until new ones grow in. When fully feathered, they show considerable tal-

ent for flying, which allows those cranes living in northern climates to spend the winter in warmer lands. This family is found on all continents except South America.

One species, the American whooping crane, *Grus americana,* has been the subject of one of the most dedicated attempts ever made to preserve a bird species from extinction. At one time, the species was reduced to 17 individual birds. But due to the efforts of bird lovers, this number has more than tripled. Now, each year, Canadian and American bird lovers anxiously await word of the migration of the whooping cranes in their hazardous journey south. They travel from northern Alberta in Canada to the Texas coast, where they spend the winter months.

The whooping crane is named for its bugle-like call, which can be heard as far as 2 miles away. These birds can measure 5 feet in height with a wing span of 7 feet.

The whooping crane builds a nest 1 to 2 feet high, on rushes in water. Not all species,

The common crane Grus grus *(left) is one of two species of crane that nests in Europe. Each winter these cranes can be seen in V-formations flying southward. The photo below shows the crowned crane.*

however, are nest builders; some simply lay their eggs in a depression in the earth.

The common crane, *Grus grus,* like the whooping crane, travels great distances to find a suitable winter climate. Nesting in the north central parts of Europe and Asia, the common crane makes its winter home in North Africa—a long-distance flight that it accomplishes in the familiar "V" formation.

The black-necked crane, *G. nigricollis,* lives in the mountains of Tibet and flies to southeast Asia for the winter. The sandhill crane, *G. canadensis,* nests in western North America and in Florida. It is becoming increasingly rare, perhaps because it is hunted locally. However, there are still about 100,000 living individuals.

One of the most beautiful cranes found in eastern Europe and throughout central Asia is the demoiselle crane, *Anthropoides virgo.* A sociable bird, it is known for its elegant plumage, with a white crest and black breast feathers providing a spectacular contrast to the gray body feathers. This bird lives and travels in impressive flocks; it win-

The moorhen, or common gallinule, Gallinula chloropus (below), is a common park bird in Europe. In America, however, it seldom leaves the shelter of marsh grasses.

ters in India and northern Africa.

A similar species, the blue, or Stanley, crane, *Tetrapteryx paradisea*, lives in South Africa. Two other African species are the wattled crane, *Bugeranus carunculatus*, and the crowned crane, *Balearica pavonina*, which is found from Senegal to Ethiopia and South Africa.

Cranes from Asia and the East include the hooded crane, *Grus monacha*, of eastern Asia; the beautiful and rare Manchurian crane, *G. japonensis*, of eastern Siberia and Japan; the Siberian white crane, *G. leucogeranus*; the white-necked crane, *G. vipio*, of southern Siberia, Korea and parts of Japan and China; the sarus crane, *G. anti-*

gone, of northern India, Thailand, and ad-
joining countries; and the Australian crane,
G. rubicunda, which is popularly called the
brolga.

The Limpkin, Aramus guarauna, is the only
member of the family Aramidae. The diet of
these birds is unusual, consisting of large
water snails, which the limpkins find in the
extensive marshes where they live.

The limpkin looks like a cross between a
crane and a rail; it is a bright, brownish-
olive color, with fine white streaks on the
neck that become larger on the rest of the
body. Even its anatomical features are characteristic of both the crane and rail families.
Sometimes known as the "wailing bird," the
limpkin's mournful, lamenting cry is heard
mostly at night.

Limpkins are found in the swamplands of
southern Georgia and Florida, through Central America, and in South America east of
the Andes to central Argentina. They also
live on numerous islands in the Caribbean.

The Trumpeters of the family Psophiidae are
residents of tropical rain forests. One of
their many curious habits is a preference
for running rather than flying. They rarely
fly, and then only with great effort. They
roost in trees at night.

Trumpeters apparently lay their eggs in
hollows, and the female is responsible for
the incubation and rearing of the young.
Little is known of their habits, primarily
because they live deep in thick, tropical
forests. However, they have been observed
taking baths in shallow water and then lying
in the sun to dry their feathers. It is also
known that trumpeters live in groups and
feed on insects, fruit, and berries, which
they gather from the forest floor. Their
name, as might be guessed, is inspired by
their hornlike call.

The trumpeter has longish legs and neck,
a short, slightly curved beak, and a round
head. The wings are rounded, and the tail
is short. Elegant black feathers decorate the
rump, and the velvety black neck plumage
has metallic reflections. These birds are the
size of domestic chickens.

The three species are the common trumpeter, Psophia crepitans; the green-winged
trumpeter, P. viridis; and the white-winged
trumpeter, P. leucoptera.

The Family Rallidae includes birds that are
mainly residents of marshes, swamps, and
bogs. This family includes the rails, coots,
gallinules, soras, and wekas. They are found
on all continents except Antarctica. There
are about 132 species in the family, which
are distributed among 45 genera.

Several U.S. members of this family are
threatened with extinction, either because of
perilously low populations or because their
habitats are threatened by change. These include the Yuma clapper rail, California clapper rail, and light-footed clapper rail, all
subspecies of Rallus longirostris; the
Hawaiian gallinule, Gallinula chloropus
sandvicensis; and the Hawaiian coot, Fulica
americana alai.

The American coot Fulica americana *(right) is a common waterbird. The white bill and blackish plumage make it easy to identify.*

A more brilliantly colored member of the family Rallidae is the husky swamphen Porphyrio porphyrio *(below). It inhabits warm regions from southern Europe through Africa and parts of Asia to Australia and New Zealand.*

The Rails are slender, and they can slip easily through bunches of marsh grass. They have compressed bodies and rather long legs and toes. They are well-adapted to life on swampy ground amid dense vegetation.

Rails can and do fly long distances. However, those that reached and settled on ocean islands have tended to lose the ability to fly. This flightless condition is probably advantageous in keeping them from being blown out to sea. However, these flightless island species, which did fly originally, have undergone great extinction. Several species have fallen victim to predators such as rats, which moved into their habitats along with man.

Shy and solitary by nature, rails prefer to move about under cover of night. Each species has its own characteristic call and song, which is often quite melodious. Rails feed on small insects and seeds. They build their nests on the ground, hidden in the marshy grass. The more aquatic coots and gallinules sometimes lodge their nests in tall grass 2 to 5 feet above water; others make nests that float like boats, rising and falling with the floods. Hatchlings are covered with a dark or black down; the adult plumage is generally a rather dull color that serves as a camouflage.

The Virginia rail, *Rallus limicola,* can be found from Canada to Central America and from the Atlantic to the Pacific. It is the best-known and most common of the dozen North American species of Rallidae. The clapper rail, *R. longirostris,* and the king rail, *R. elegans,* are two other widely distributed species.

The water rail, *R. aquaticus,* has the widest distribution of the family; it is found from the northernmost parts of Europe eastward to Asia and south to Arabia and Africa. The trademark of the water rail is a long, slightly curved red bill.

The cape rail, *R. caerulescens,* lives throughout most of Africa; the blue-breasted banded rail, *R. striatus,* is common from southern Asia eastward to the Philippine Islands; the banded rail, *R. philippensis,* and the barred rail, *R. torquatus,* also inhabit the Philippines, as well as nearby islands.

The Sora, or **Sora Rail,** *Porzana carolina,* is found in North America. In Europe and part of middle Asia there are closely related species. These are the spotted crake, *P. porzana;* the little crake, *P. parva;* and Baillon's crake, *P. pusilla.*

The Weka, *Gallirallus australis,* lives in New Zealand. It seems to have mastered the technique of survival against enormous odds. This pullet-sized, flightless rail has managed to resist the onslaught of the rats, cats, and dogs that came to the island with man, wreaking havoc on the eggs of ground-nesting birds.

The weka is completely flightless. It uses its wings for balance only, racing through lowland forests at night and making fast ground-level attacks on crickets, mice, and the eggs of other birds.

The Gallinules are members of the genus *Gallinula.* Also known as waterhens or water chickens, most of these birds are slate gray in color and are about the size of bantam chickens.

The purple gallinule, *Porphyrula martinica,* is one of the most beautiful marsh birds in North America. Unlike most other Rallidae, it is very highly colored. It has purple

plumage, a crimson bill, a cobalt-blue shield (a horny prolongation of the bill) on its forehead, and bright yellow legs.

The Coots are placed in the genus *Fulica.* They are good swimmers, but slow flyers; hunters shoot them only when ducks are not available. These birds multiply rapidly and, like the gallinules, lay their eggs at the rate of one a day.

The common coot, *F. atra,* is found in Europe. In this species there are lobes on each side of the toes to assist in swimming.

Coots, unlike other rails, spend much time swimming. As can be seen in this photo of a European coot, they sometimes nest on the branches of fallen trees along lakeshores and riverbanks. Coots lay a large clutch of white eggs, speckled with black.

The American coot, *F. americana,* is found throughout most of the Americas, while the horned coot, *F. cornuta,* lives around high mountain lakes of the Andes of South America. The horned coot has the strange habit of building its nest in the center of a lake on an artificial island that it makes out of large quantities of vegetation or—most interestingly—stones. Another peculiarity of the horned coot is its frontal wattles, the "horns" that give the bird its name. These wattles increase in size during the mating season, although it seems that they are the same size in both males and females.

Living in the same general Andean region, but more northerly, is the giant coot, *F. gigantea.* This bird deserves its name, for it is the largest species of *Fulica,* attaining a length of some 20 inches. Like the horned coot, it builds nests in mountain lakes, but only of vegetation.

The Finfoots belong to the family Heliornithidae. These birds are appropriately named, for they are superb swimmers and divers.

Finfoots are longer and slimmer than rails, and have longer and more functional tails. They have flaps on their toes to assist them in swimming. They also resemble divers in certain of their aquatic habits. They live in thick equatorial forests along lake shores and river banks, a location that makes scientific observation of their habits difficult.

All three species of this family have an almost rigid tail, a knob at the joint nearest the body in the folded wing, and legs that are curiously colored—the American species has zebra-striped legs. The finfoot has a little pouch under each wing. The two chicks are carried in these pouches, one under each wing, as the parent swims.

The males, which are duller in color than the females, take care of incubation and the education of the young. Only the eggs of the African species have ever been seen—they are rather small and cream-colored. The simply constructed nests are built on the branches of trees.

The smallest finfoot, *Heliornis fulica,* is found from Mexico to Argentina. *Heliopais personata,* which is twice as big, is distributed from Assam to Malaysia. The largest of the finfoots, *Podica senegalensis,* lives in Africa.

The Sunbittern, *Eurypyga helias,* is the only species of the family Eurypygidae. It measures more than 20 inches in length.

When it spreads its wings in display, two impressive chestnut crescents blaze forth

from a bright orange halo. The sunbittern's name is derived from this resemblance to the sun setting in a dark sky.

It has a sturdy, graceful body with a long neck and long legs. The head is a striking contrast of black and white. A white stripe runs over each eye and two additional white stripes mark the cheeks. Neck, shoulders, and breast are brown, but the throat, belly, and region under the tail are creamy white. The rest of the plumage is olive brown with black and white spots, and the longish tail is decorated by two broad black bands.

Sunbitterns are silent birds; one rarely hears their melancholy whistle. Retiring in their habits, they generally stay by themselves, or perhaps with a mate. They live on the dense, forested banks of streams and rivers, from Mexico to Bolivia and central Brazil.

The Seriemas, or **Cariamas,** are members of the family Cariamidae. There are only two species—the crested seriema, *Cariama cristata*, and the Burmeister's, or black-legged, seriema, *Chunga burmeisteri*. These long-legged birds live exclusively in South America.

For many years, there was a popular belief that the seriemas were immune to rattlesnake bites. However, modern experiments have proved the contrary. Weak doses of diluted snake venom were injected into captured seriemas, and they soon died. The birds apparently have survived attacks by snakes mainly because they are sufficiently agile to escape. Furthermore, they seem to have an instinct that enables them to distinguish between poisonous snakes and the harmless species that they capture for food. Seriemas also feed on lizards and insects.

The Kagu, *Rhynochetes jubatus*, is the sole representative of the family Rhynochetidae. Any person who has ever seen even a stuffed specimen of the kagu is fortunate, because

31

it is rare and nearly extinct. Found only in New Caledonia, the kagu is equal in size to the ordinary hen, but it has longer legs, sparcer plumage, a dark gray color, and a disheveled crest on its head. When it spreads its wings, however, and displays a rather splendid design of black, white and reddish patches, its dullness disappears and it looks strikingly like the sunbittern. The red coloration of the kagu's legs and beak add to the strangeness of the bird's appearance.

The Bustards are members of the family Otididae. There are 22 species of bustards, which are found mainly in Africa; they are also found in Europe, Asia, and Australia. In the bustards, the feet have only three front toes, and are well-adapted for rapid walking and running. The large, long wings give good leverage for flight.

Some bustards are among the largest of the flying birds. The male is fancifully adorned with crests, ruffs, and collars that are prominently displayed during courtship. Some species have inflatable pouches on the throat, which serve as echo chambers for their deep mating cries. The female is un-adorned and spends her time at home incubating eggs.

Water Birds— Charadriiformes

The order Charadriiformes includes 3 sub-orders with 16 families. Many of these birds, such as the woodcocks and snipes, are widely hunted. Some of the other charadriiformes are plovers, lapwings, gulls, terns, sand-pipers, stilts, curlews, and auks.

Superficially, certain of the species seem to have little relation to each other—the snipe and the gull, for instance, or the lap-wing and the guillemot. However, on the basis of anatomical evidence, these birds are similar enough to group into one order.

The Shore Birds are all included in the sub-order Charadrii. Most of these birds live close to water, particularly in marshy areas, and along the sandy and muddy shores of both fresh and salt water. They are skillful and swift in flight, but prefer to depend upon their natural camouflage for protection, instead of flying away from approaching danger.

In most species, the beak is long, slender, and well-adapted to capturing the worms, insects, and small shellfish that constitute the normal diet. Most species are migratory, and some make transoceanic or transcontinental trips in search of warm weather. Many nest on the arctic tundra.

The Charadriidae and Scolopacidae are the two most important and most widely distributed families in this suborder.

The Plovers and Lapwings belong to the family Charadriidae, which contains about 60 species. The species are divided into two groups—true plovers and lapwings. Both groups have combinations of black, white, and sand-brown plumage. This coloration provides excellent comouflage by breaking up the bulk of the body so that in certain landscapes it no longer looks like part of a bird. Some species have a white band on the back of the neck, and a dark band on the chest and tail.

The lapwings include about 24 species. All have a tail that is white at the base, frequently with a black band. The main feathers of the wings are always black and often have a broad horizontal white stripe. Many lapwings have crests of varying length on the back of the neck, facial wattles, and spurs on the wings. The wings are often quite broad and rounded. Many species are found in Africa, but lapwings also occur in Europe, Asia, Australia, and South America. Lapwings are often found far from water.

The common lapwing *Vanellus vanellus*, is one of the best-known species. It nests in England, where hard-boiled lapwing eggs were once a favorite hors d'oeuvre.

In the Orient, the best-known species are the red-wattled lapwing, *V. indicus*, and the yellow-wattled lapwing, *V. malabaricus*. The most widely distributed species in South America is the southern lapwing, *V. chilensis*, which is found over most of the continent. Australia is the home of the three-colored lapwing, *V. tricolor*, and two subspecies of the masked lapwing, *V. miles*.

The spurred lapwing, *Hoplopterus spinosus*, lives in southeast Europe, the African tropics, and the Middle East. It has wing spurs. Its African counterpart is the very similar blacksmith plover, *H. armatus*.

Another species that occasionally reaches Europe is the sociable lapwing, *Chettusa gregaria*. It nests in a limited area of the Ural region in the U.S.S.R.

The plovers include 5 genera with about 26 species. The golden plovers of the genus *Pluvialis* have a plumage that is uncharac-

teristic of the family—the white bar on the back of the neck is lacking, and the upper parts are delicately spotted rather than solid. They have black underparts during the mating season. Although they are only the size of a robin and usually do not rest on the surface of the water, golden plovers are able to fly nonstop from eastern Canada to South America—a distance of almost 2,500 miles. On arrival they have lost only about 2 ounces in weight.

The ordinary golden plover, *Pluvialis apricaria*, nests in northern Europe and the northwest part of Asia, migrating in the autumn to reach the Mediterranean regions and India. The arctic areas of North America and eastern Siberia are the home of similar species. One such species is the American, or lesser, golden plover, *P. dominica*, which is particularly well-known for lengthy migrations. Some subspecies travel as far as Australia and Argentina, while the Alaskan birds usually winter in Hawaii. The gray, or black-

The black-winged lapwing (above) belongs to a populous group of African plovers. Closely related to the European lapwing, it has darker feathers and a thread-thin tuft at the back of its neck.

bellied, plover, *P. squatarola,* is an arctic bird that travels as far as Chile, Australia, and South Africa.

The New Zealand dotterel, *P. obscurus,* which is found only in that country, is apparently not migratory.

The genus *Charadrius* includes small or medium-sized plovers with brown or sand-gray coloring above and white below. One or two dark bands cross the breast and another descends from the eye to the beak. There are more than 20 species in this genus.

The ringed plover, *C. hiaticula,* is a coastal species found in Europe and Asia. Its North American counterpart is the semipalmated plover, *C. semipalmatus,* which some regard as the same species. Other very similar

European species include the little ringed plover, *C. dubius,* and the snowy plover, *C. alexandrinus,* which has many subspecies.

The killdeer, *C. vociferus,* inhabits inland areas of North America and the northwestern coast of South America. It lacks the white neck band but is decorated with two breast stripes.

Like the killdeer, the three-banded plover, *C. tricollaris,* has two breast stripes. This bird is a native of tropical Africa and Madagascar. The Caspian plover, *C. asiaticus,* is found on Asian steppes. The mountain plover, *C. montanus,* is found on dry plateaus bordering the Rocky Mountains; it, too, lacks the white band on the back of the neck. Surprisingly, the mountain plover does not

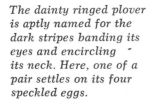

The dainty ringed plover is aptly named for the dark stripes banding its eyes and encircling its neck. Here, one of a pair settles on its four speckled eggs.

34

The Kentish, or snowy, plover Charadrius alexandrinus *is small and pale. This is a widespread species with many subspecies.*

live near water at any time of the year.

Many other species of plovers are found in Africa, Asia, and Australia. New Zealand is the home of the most unusual of these birds, the wry-bill plover, *Anarhynchus frontalis*—it has a beak that is curved to the right. This adaptation appears to suit very well the feeding habits of the wry-bill, sometimes called the crook-bill plover. This bird feeds on beach insects that hide under rocks and must be extracted.

Curlews, Sandpipers, Woodcocks, Snipes, and Ruffs are familiar members of the family Scolopacidae. Woodcocks and snipes are especially familiar game birds throughout the world. In the past members of the smaller species were shot and cooked to make "peep pie." However, these birds are no longer regarded as game. There are about 80 species in this family.

The family Scolopacidae includes a variety of shore birds. Their lengths, including bills, vary from 5 to 28 inches. Well-adapted to

flying, the wings are long and rather pointed. The legs and neck are long, as is the slender beak, which may be straight or curved. Their frequently mottled plumage combines browns, grays, and whites. Most scolopacids live in northern regions—some are even found in the vicinity of the North Pole— and they migrate to warmer weather in winter.

In both their winter and summer homes, scolopacids select areas of low-growing grass and bushes around swamps or other bodies of water. Their long, sensitive beaks enable them to capture the tiny crabs, worms, and other invertebrates on which they feed. Highly sociable except in the nesting period, the Scolopacidae often join groups composed of different species. Many have melodious songs, and some produce interesting sounds with their wings. Their courtship rituals tend to be quite complicated.

Generally, the Scolopacidae nest on the ground, although one or two species use off-the-ground nests built by other birds. The typical nest is a hole partially lined with grass and large enough to hold the common clutch of four beautiful, pointed eggs. The precocious newly-hatched fledglings immediately leave the nest with their parents.

The Curlews, members of the genus *Numenius,* include some of the largest scolopacids. These birds are characterized by a downward curving beak. The Eskimo curlew, *N. borealis,* of North America, is almost extinct; the slender-billed curlew, *N. tenuirostris,* which nests in marshy steppes in Asia, is extremely rare.

The most widely scattered species are the common curlew, *N. arquata,* found from Europe east to the Himalayas; its North American counterpart, the long-billed curlew, *N. americanus;* and the whimbrel, or Hudsonian curlew, *N. phaeopus,* which breeds in the Arctic.

The Sandpipers, like the plovers, hold records for long-distance migratory flights. Two species, the white-rumped sandpiper, *Erolia fuscicollis,* and Baird's sandpiper, *E. bairdii,* travel from the northernmost areas of North America to the beaches of Patagonia at the southern tip of South America. The white-rumped sandpiper, however, travels over the Atlantic Ocean, while Baird's sandpiper flies overland.

Other members of the large, northern genus *Erolia* are the Old World curlew sandpiper and little stint, as well as the tiny least sandpiper, which is only 6 inches long.

The genus *Tringa* includes several species of sandpipers, most of which live in the temperate zones. The best known are the greenshank, *T. nebularia,* the redshank, *T. totanus,* the spotted redshank, *T. erythropus,* the green sandpiper, *T. ochropus,* and the wood sandpiper, *T. glareola*—all Old World species. The greater yellowlegs, *T. melanoleuca,* and the lesser yellowlegs, *T. flavipes,* are found in North America.

The common sandpiper, *Actitis hypoleucos,* and the spotted sandpiper, *A. macularia,* are two very similar species with separate areas of distribution. The first is Eurasian, while the second is North American. They are identifiable by their tendency to bob up and down between steps—perhaps this enables the bird to formulate depth perception and perspective on the flat shore. The spotted sandpiper's breast is highly spotted, but only in the courtship plumage.

Woodcocks and Snipes are members of the subfamily Scolopacinae. The Asian woodcock, *Scolopax rusticola,* is widely distributed in the Old World; there are sedentary related species in the hilly areas of Indonesia and New Guinea. The North American woodcock, *Philohela minor,* is similar to the Asian woodcock, but smaller. It has long been a favorite game bird and is also known for its remarkable evening flight song.

Snipes are native to almost all parts of the world except Australia and southern Asia. However, even these areas may be temporary homes for some species during the migratory season. The best-known species of all the snipes is the common snipe. *Capella gallinago.* The jack snipe, *Lymnocryptes minima,* is another Old World species. New Zealand is the home of one species, *Coenocorypha aucklandica.*

The Godwits of the genus *Limosa* are large sandpipers with proportionately longer beaks and legs than snipes. The black-tailed godwit, *L. limosa,* and the bar-tailed godwit, *L. lapponica,* are two Old World species. Two others, the marbled godwit, *L. fedoa,* and the hudsonian godwit, *L. haemastica,* are New World.

The ruff, *Philomachus pugnax,* is found from northern France to Siberia. This species is characterized by marked differences between the sexes. The males are larger than the females, and develop an ornamental plumage of collars, ruffs, and other neck adornments during the mating season. These are flaunted during elaborate parades that are held in a suitable arena, or display area. This territory, selected and defined by the males, is not far from the nest ground. Here the males engage in sometimes bloody combat to establish their rights over favored breeding sites. After mating, the females are left alone to incubate the eggs and take care of the young.

The stint (above), grubbing for food, is a tiny sandpiper. With its long, sensitive beak, it probes the mud for tiny snails or larvae.

Unlike most shorebirds, the Eurasian woodcock (right) prefers brushy swamps and the leafy forest floor. Its markings match this habitat.

The Phalaropes of the family Phalaropodidae are closely related to the Scolopacidae. This group includes three northern species of sea-going birds. Female phalaropes are more brightly colored than males; and it is the female phalarope that does the courting. The smaller male (the birds are from 6 to 8 inches long) builds the nest, incubates the eggs, and cares for the young.

Wilson's phalarope, *Steganopus tricolor*, winters along the western coasts of North and South America. During the summer it is often seen at inland lakes of the United States. The northern phalarope, *Lobipes lobatus*, is sometimes seen in the United States. It breeds in the Arctic. The red phalarope, *Phalaropus fulicarius*, is also an Arctic breeder, but found even farther north.

The Jacanas are members of the family Jacanidae. There are seven species of jacanas, in tropical regions. They are moderate-sized birds, and may be up to 14 inches long. Their bodies are rather compact and their wings rounded. In most species the tails are short.

The long legs and very long toes bear a certain resemblance to those of the purple gallinule. The jacanas are capable of hopping among the floating vegetation of the tropical rivers, lakes, and marshes in which they live. Also known as lily-trotters, they are fair swimmers and divers. They generally establish their nests in floating vegetation. As a rule, the nest holds four eggs, brown or yellow, which are so highly polished that they look varnished.

The Painted Snipes are members of the family Rostratulidae. The two species are reminiscent of the snipe in shape, but have a beautiful bronze plumage with a number of light areas that are much more contrasting in the female than in the male.

Rostratula benghalensis is very widely distributed throughout the tropical and neotropical zones of Africa, Asia, and Australia. *Nycticryphes semicollaris* is limited to South America. In both species, the more brilliant plumage of the female goes hand-in-hand with the reversed roles of the sexes, as the male assumes the responsibility for incubating and rearing the young.

The Oystercatchers belong to the family Haematopodidae. This family has only one genus, Haematopus, which contains from four to perhaps seven species. Oystercatchers are adorned with elegant black and (usually) white feathers, against which the powerful beak and the glowing pink legs stand out. The shape of the beak is well-adapted for dealing with oysters, which constitute the major part of the diet. They also feed on other shellfish, worms, and insects.

The common oystercatcher, *H. ostralegus*, is a shore bird, although it may also nest along inland waterways. It is nearly worldwide in range. Other species can be found in the Southern Hemisphere.

The Avocets and Stilts are members of the family Recurvirostridae. The avocets belong to the genus *Recurvirostra*. Other members of the family are the common stilt, *Himantopus himantopus*; the banded stilt, *Cladorhynchus leucocephala*; and the ibisbill, *Ibidorhyncha struthersii*. They are all characterized by a slender, upward-curving beak.

The avocets have partly webbed feet that enable them to wade in shallow water, especially the brackish water where they like to feed and nest. The common avocet, *R. avosetta*, nests from Europe eastward. The beautiful American avocet, *R. americana*, nests around brackish lakes in the western United States, while the Chilean avocet, *R. andina*, is found in bodies of brackish waters

Both birds seen on this page are remarkable for their individuality. The ruff (below left) is unique in that no two males garbed in their breeding plumage are exactly alike.

The black-tailed godwit (below right) varies in size, length of beak, and coloring from others of its species.

in the Andes Mountains. Australia and New Zealand are the homes of the red-necked avocet, *R. novaehollandiae*.

The legs of the common stilt permit it to wade in shallow water. In flight, the legs extend well beyond the tail, giving the birds an unmistakable silhouette that is outlined by the black feathers on top of the wings and the white ones beneath. The common stilt is found in both the New and Old Worlds.

The Stone-curlews include nine species of the family Burhinidae. They are also known as thicknees. Seven species belong to genus *Burhinus* and one each to *Esacus* and *Orthorhamphus*.

Stone-curlews reach a length of 21 inches. Their legs are quite long, and they have only three short frontal toes. Their heads are large, with relatively short, sturdy beaks and huge yellow eyes well-adapted to night hunting. In all species, the plumage—a light brown base with fine tracings and wider dark striping—provides good camouflage. Most species are African, but the common stone-curlew, *B. oedicnemus*, reaches England.

The Crab-plover, *Dromas ardeola*, is placed in its own family, Dramadidae. Closely re-

The oystercatcher (right) is well named. The bird's slender bill can be plunged like a dagger in partly opened oyster shells, paralyzing the oyster before it can clamp its shell.

lated to the stone-curlews, it is a peculiar coastal species of Africa and southwestern Asia.

The Coursers and Pratincoles comprise the family Glareolidae. The coursers have a uniform coloring, often with a chest band. They resemble the stone-curlews and the plovers. Coursers are small and live in open country. The best-known are the cream-colored courser, *Cursorius cursor*, sometimes found in Europe, and the crocodile bird, *Pluvianus aegyptius*. The other courser species belong to the genera *Rhinoptilus* and *Peltohyas*.

The crocodile bird is a beautiful gray above and a cream color below; there is a prominent dark green stripe running the length of the beak to the back of the neck. This bird derives its name from its reputation for searching the inside of crocodiles' mouths for tiny food leftovers. However, this daring act, first mentioned by the Greek historian Herodotus in the 5th century B.C., has yet to be confirmed.

The pratincoles, or swallow-plovers, resemble the coursers in coloring. In shape, however, they are like terns and have a similarly forked tail. In Africa, pratincoles are known also as locust birds because of

The stone-curlew (left) is also called the thick-knee. It inhabits rocky plains and is active at night.

their habit of following migratory hordes of these insects.

Species of pratincoles are found throughout most of the world, with the exception of the Americas. Three species belong to genus *Glareola*, three to *Galachrysia*, and one to *Stiltia*.

The Seed-snipes of the family Thinocoridae are found only in South America. This family includes four species of small and medium-sized birds whose plumage resembles that of the quail. Seed-snipes have long, pointed wings, relatively short tails, and very short legs. Their short, conical beaks are equipped for plucking up seeds, which are their main food. Their rapid, zigzag flight is reminiscent of the snipe. Seed-snipes typically inhabit dry regions, from the high Andes to the Pacific coast.

Seed-snipes nest on the ground. Their eggs are dove-colored and splashed with tiny lilac or chocolate spots. The white-bellied seed-snipe, *Attagis malouinus*, builds its nest in the mountains. Its eggs, decorated with sharply contrasting colors, blend in with the environment, which is rich in lichens.

The Sheathbills of the family Chionididae are found in the region of the South Pole. There are two species in the single genus *Chionis*.

Sheathbills are about 16 inches long and have completely white plumage. They look remarkably like doves. They eat both small invertebrates and the algae and organic refuse washed up on beaches by the sea. They also are scavengers in the rookeries of seals and penguins. Their primitive nests are built among rocks and fissures, often near colonies of penguins.

The Suborder Lari includes the gulls; the graceful terns noted for their long migrations; the piratical skuas, which raid other members of the suborder; and the skimmers. This suborder has a vast distribution through-out the world, including the Arctic and the edge of the Antarctic.

Unlike the typical Charadriiformes, the Lari have webbed feet. Although considered birds of the sea, most gulls and terns remain quite close to the shoreline.

The Skuas of the family Stercorariidae are similar to gulls in shape and size, but have dark plumage. They obtain their food by pirating it from gulls, terns, and other marine birds. Skuas fly after the other birds and force them to drop the food they are carrying in their beaks. The skuas catch the food in midair. They also prey on small birds on the wing.

With its short, rather stubby tail, the great skua would appear to be an awkward flier. This is not the case, however; this bird can fly very swiftly. This facility, of course, makes possible the great skua's aerial feeding habits.

The great skua, *Catharacta skua*, is uniformly brown with small light spots. It is the size of a herring gull, but heavier. The various breeds of this species are found in the polar regions. They breed in Iceland

The pratincole (right) has a bib of black and white feathers. These birds are distributed throughout the Old World.

42

and the Shetland Islands. They nest in small groups, often near colonies of other marine birds (particularly penguins in the Antarctic), which they often rob of both eggs and young.

The three other species of skuas are known as jaegers. They are the parasitic jaeger, *Stercorarius parasiticus,* the long-tailed jaeger, *S. longicaudatus,* and the pomarine jaeger, *S. pomarinus.*

More agile than the great skua, the jaegers have two stabilizing feathers in the centers of the tail. The feathers are short in the parasitic jaeger and prominent in the other two species. The pomarine jaeger's central tail feathers are broad and turned up rather than pointed and threadlike. The plumage of these species has two phases, one dark and one light; in the pomarine jaeger, the lower parts are cream white rather than brown. The jaegers nest on the arctic tundra and winter at sea farther south.

Skuas and jaegers both incubate in depressions on the ground. Generally they lay two eggs. Those of the skua are dun-colored with dark spots; the jaegers' eggs are sometimes greenish, also with dark spots.

The stone-curlew (above) has a large head and a short, sturdy beak. Its large yellow eyes are well adapted for hunting at night.

The crocodile plover (far left) was once believed to get food from the inside of crocodile's mouths.

The white sheathbill (left) lives only in the Antarctic. It often builds its nest near colonies of penguins.

The black-legged kitti-wake (opposite page) is a gull named for its call. It lives in large colonies on coastal cliffs in northern waters.

Gulls and Terns belong to the family Laridae. The gulls are the familiar sea birds found around seaports; the terns resemble gulls but are smaller. Laridae range in length from 8 to 32 inches, and have strong bodies and long, pointed wings. The tails are generally squared in the gulls and forked in the terns. The sturdy beak is compressed at the sides. Most species are white, with the wings and back in varying shades of gray.

Gulls generally nest in colonies along the shoreline or on the least-accessible islands. They build rough nests of grass and twigs among the rocks or on grassy or sandy soil. They occasionally nest in freshwater marsh areas or in trees. One to four eggs are laid in the nest and incubated by both parents;

both parents care for the young during the time they remain in the nest. In species that build their nests on steep cliffs, the young do not leave the nest at all until they are fully capable of flying. The plumage of the young gull is almost always a mottled brown. The adult plumage is acquired only after several years, with the exact time depending on the species.

Gulls hunt for their food in flocks. Marvelous fliers, they space themselves over a wide area of water. When one of them sights food—almost any variety of garbage, or, less often, fish—its actions serve as a signal to the others in the group. All of them then swoop down, converging to feed. They float and swim easily, even in rough seas.

The swallow-tailed gull (right) is a native of the Galapagos Islands. The only gull that is active at night, it spends the time hunting small squids.

Seldom do gulls submerge much of their bodies as they chase and fight over food.

These birds are also quite capable of moving quickly and easily on land. Occasionally they run or walk after the plow, gleaning whatever they can. On land, gulls stalk and devour grasshoppers, too.

Some species of gulls feed on young sea turtles and hard-shelled mollusks. They manage this by battering their prey against hard surfaces, like large rocks or concrete pavements, to break the shells. Other gulls customarily rob other birds' nests—and sometimes nests of their own species—of eggs and even chicks.

The white-headed and hooded gulls belong to the genus *Larus*. A typical white-headed gull is the herring gull, *L. argentatus*. In the hooded gulls the adult has a dark hood that extends over its head during the mating season. This is found in the black-headed gull, *L. ridibundus*. This genus also includes an unusual Galapagos species, the forked-tailed gull, *L. furcatus*.

Franklin's gull, *L. pipixcan*, has a special place among North American gulls because it is the only one that spends winters south of the equator. This gull mates in North American prairie swamps but mi-

Caspian terns (opposite, above) rest on the sand of a beach during their migration period.

A half-grown black-headed gull (opposite, below) displays its winter plumage. By summer, it will no longer have black bars on its tail but will wear a kind of dark "hood" on its head.

Two photos of a pair of great skuas (top right and bottom right) show the quarrelsome nature of these piratelike relatives of the gulls.

The lara gull (bottom left) inhabits the rocky Galapagos Islands off the west coast of South America.

grates to South America. Black headed, with a white neck and grey back, Franklin's gull is about 15 inches in length. Its feeding habits are beneficial to man because insects —chiefly grasshoppers—are its staple.

Another insect-eating species, the California gull, *L. californicus,* is the state bird of Utah—and there is a monument to the gull in Salt Lake City. This bird was thus honored by the Mormon founders of Utah because, in the early days, huge flocks of gulls appeared to devour the grasshoppers that were devastating the pioneers' crops. The gull saved the settlers from starvation and so earned its place as a state symbol.

The little gull, *L. minutus,* is the smallest member of the subfamily Larinae, which comprises the gulls. This bird is a bit less than a foot long. It is found in the Old World, but sometimes it is also seen in

eastern Canada and the eastern United
States. The largest of the gulls is a North
American species, the great black-backed
gull. It is 32 inches in length; this bird's
wingspread exceeds 5 feet.

Ross's gull, *Rhodostethia rosea*, is one of
the least-known species. It builds its nests
exclusively in northern Siberia, has a finely
striped tail, a small black collar, and a beautiful pink shading in its plumage.

The terns resemble gulls in many respects
but are generally smaller, slimmer, and have
longer wings. Most terns have white plumage, although the wings and back are often
gray, and the top of the head is frequently
dark during the mating period. The beak is
generally quite long and narrow. The legs,
which have three forward toes joined by a
membrane, are rather short. The color of
the beak and legs is often red or yellow,
with seasonal variations.

Terns' habits are similar to those of the
gulls. However, unlike gulls, many species
of terns hunt by diving from considerable
heights, straight down into the water in an
unerring line to capture fish or other aquatic
life. They are also more at home on the open
sea, and nest on many oceanic islands that
lack gulls.

Terns are remarkably gregarious and often
nest in great colonies. Most make their nests
on the ground, digging a hole in the sand
or gravel, or in the shelter of plants. The
freshwater species builds floating nests. Terns
are also cosmopolitan in their distribution,
but some species are typical of fresh water
and are found along the coast or over salt
water only during migration. Unlike gulls,
they are not scavengers.

Some sand-nesting terns have a remarkable capacity. They lay their eggs—usually
three—in a depression that they have hol-

lowed out in the sand. Afterward, the eggs are sometimes covered during sandstorms. But the parent birds have no difficulty at all in finding the hidden eggs. In fact, experiments have confirmed that even when the eggs are totally covered by wind-blown sand and there are no visible identifying clues to their location, the adult terns are not in the least confused. They discover the buried eggs without hesitation. Scientists haven't yet explained this ability.

The white tern, or fairy tern, *Gygis alba*, is a species noted for its peculiar breeding habits. Its single egg is generally laid on a bare tree branch, and the bird incubates it in this uncomfortable position. This interesting tern, which is distributed over the warm oceans of the world, has plumage that is completely white.

Perhaps the most beautiful species is the Inca tern, *Larosterna inca*, which is found on the west coast of South America. Its plumage is slate-colored, its beak and legs scarlet. Two clusters of slender white feathers spring out from the sides of the head.

The Skimmers belong to the family Rynchopidae. The three species of skimmers boast a unique and extremely efficient beak, well-adapted to fishing. It is shorter on the top than on the bottom, and is compressed at the sides. The lower part is flexible and is equipped with small blades that plow through the water and capture fish and other aquatic animals just below the surface. The top part then clamps down to block the escape of the prey.

Skimmers prefer the calm waters of rivers and estuaries. Their nests are simply depressions in the sand, in which two to four handsome, spotted eggs are laid. The young can run and swim as soon as they have hatched. The two sections of the beak are equal in length at birth.

The black skimmer, *Rhynchops nigra*, lives along the coasts and rivers of the temperate and tropical regions of the Americas. The African skimmer, R. *flavirostris*, and the Indian skimmer, R. *albicollis*, are found, respectively, on the large rivers of Africa and southern Asia.

The long-beaked marsh, or black, tern (above) prefers the brackish, still waters of inland Italy. It nests in the rice fields of the Po Valley.

The penguinlike razor-billed auks (above left) are coastal sea birds of the North Atlantic. They lay a single spotted egg in a crevice in the rocks.

49

Puffins (right) are members of the auk family. The brilliantly colored sections of the beak drop off after the mating season. Puffins live in colonies with auks, murres, and some species of gull. One such colony, in the Bering Sea near Alaska, is reputed to be the largest bird colony in North America. The birds shown here are common puffins of the North Atlantic Ocean.

The Suborder Alcae includes the auks, puffins, razorbills, and guillemots.

The auks closely resemble the penguins of the Southern Hemisphere. Like penguins, auks are clumsy on land but completely at ease in the water. They inhabit coastal areas where they nest in colonies among the rocks or on reefs.

Auks swim and dive with great skill, using both their webbed feet and short wings—which serve as fins—to propel themselves through the water. They eat the fish, mollusks, and other marine life that they capture beneath the surface of the water. Auks measure from 6 to 32 inches in length. Unlike penguins, most of them can fly.

This suborder contains only one family, the Alcidae, and all species tend to nest in colonies on seaside cliffs and offshore islands. Auks, puffins, razorbills, and guillemots of this family may all live together as members of one community, dividing the available space on the cliff.

The great auk, *Pinguinus impennis*, was probably the first North American bird to be totally destroyed by European man. The last

two birds were seen in 1844 off the coast of Iceland, where they were killed and their single egg smashed, thus eliminating a species that had been hunted by man for over 300 years.

The razorbill, *Alca torda*, has a broad, compressed beak.

The genus *Uria* includes three species, all known as murres or guillemots.

Another group in the suborder Alcae is the distinctive puffins, which are identifiable by their strange beaks. The beaks have a number of horny appendages that vanish after the hatching season.

The sandgrouse (above), a migrant bird, is a favorite target of game hunters. Some species that live in cold climates have feathered legs.

Sandgrouse (below left) pause at a waterhole. These birds are often shot as they fly in to drink.

Guillemots, known as murres in North America (below right), live in densely packed colonies. They are members of the auk family.

Terrestrial and Arboreal Birds—Columbiformes

The order Columbiformes includes sandgrouse, pigeons, and doves. Dodos and solitaires were also members of this group, but these birds are now extinct.

This order is divided into two main families. The members of both groups may be similar in appearance, but they differ greatly in their habits and distribution. The families Pteroclidae, the sandgrouse, and Columbidae, the pigeons and doves, have similar vocal organs; a well-developed sternum, or breastbone; thick plumage; and long, pointed wings. Both groups have a swift, even style of flight, and they drink by sucking water without lifting their heads.

The Sandgrouse, because of their rigid habits, have fallen victim to game hunters. These birds gather at regular hours, frequently in huge flocks, at established locations to drink water. They sometimes fly 70 or 80 miles to the source of the water. This habit enables man to find and kill them. If their habits were not so predictable, the sandgrouse might well escape because they are naturally very shy and wary. Also, their plumage is marked by fine tracery lines and dark patches and bands; these markings break up their form and permit them to blend in with the background. Their wings and tail are longer and more pointed than those of the pigeon. The central tail feathers, in particular, are long and thin, and their short legs have feathery toes.

The nest is a mere depression in the soil where the female lays three eggs. She incubates them by day, and the male cares for them at night. The newborn have down feathers and resemble downy chicks. They can leave the nest immediately after hatching, but the parents continue to provide re-

The diamond dove (opposite page) is a small Australian species and a favorite of aviculturists (people who raise birds).

gurgitated food. The adults live almost entirely on seeds. Unlike any other birds, some sandgrouse can carry water to their nestlings in special absorbent breast feathers.

The genus *Syrrhaptes* contains the common sandgrouse, *S. paradoxus*, and the Tibetan sandgrouse, *S. tibetanus*. Both species inhabit the desert and arid regions of the steppes and mountains of central Asia. The Tibetan sandgrouse remains in its natural habitat, but the common sandgrouse occasionally migrates, usually toward the west. One of the most spectacular migrations was in 1908, when flocks of them reached England, France, and Italy.

The genus *Pterocles* includes 14 species that are found chiefly in Africa and Asia. However, one species, the large pin-tailed sandgrouse, *P. alchata*, lives in southern Europe. This genus was thought to have its origins in Africa, but ancient fossils have recently been found in various parts of Europe and Asia as well.

The Pigeons, of all domestic birds, have the greatest number of breeds and varieties. These include such types as the pouter; the fantail, which has a wheel-shaped tail; and the hooded pigeon, which has very long curved feathers on its head. All pigeons evolved from the same wild species, the wild pigeon, or rock dove, *Columba livia*. The turtledove, whose attentions to its mate are legendary, was bred by man and was originally an Afro-Asian species.

The domestic and semidomestic pigeons are so plentiful in the cities of the world that they sometimes cause considerable sanitary and health problems. They can carry viruses that cause diseases, such as psittacosis, which can be transmitted to humans.

The family Columbidae consists of about 280 species of pigeons and doves, divided into 43 genera. They inhabit every part of the world except the Arctic and Antarctic. They vary greatly in size. The body is usually

compact and robust, with short legs. The head is small and rounded; the short beak is bare, often with a fleshy mound over the nostrils. The plumage of the males is usually similar to that of the females.

Nearly all species are tree dwellers, but a few are earthbound or rock dwellers. For the most part, they fly very well. Pigeons are often migratory and sociable in their habits, even during the nesting season.

Their diet consists of seeds, fruits, berries, buds, and in some cases, insects. Their nests are simple, solid constructions of interwoven twigs, even among those species, like the wild pigeon, that nest among rocks or in caves. Depending upon the species, pigeons lay one or two eggs at a time; these are incubated by both sexes. Males and females both produce "pigeon milk", a substance secreted by the lining of the parents' crop, which is the sole food of the very young bird for about a week.

The Subfamily Columbinae includes not only the most typical pigeons and doves, but also the quail dove of Central and South America, the pheasant pigeon of New Guinea, various small South American forms, and the bronze-winged pigeon of Australia. This subfamily includes the large genus *Columba* and many others, such as *Streptopelia, Geotrygon,* and *Otidiphaps.*

Although the coloration can be diverse, most species in this subfamily have various color combinations, modulated in gray, brown, and wine, with iridescent areas and black or white neck feathers. The wings and tail are prominent both in flight and in courting displays. Most Columbinae are grain eaters. Some species, including the common turtledove, *Streptopelia turtur,* and the wood pigeon, *Columba palumbus,* are migratory.

The rock dove is still widely distributed in Europe, western Asia, India, and North Africa. It lives in the rocks of mountains or

Fruit pigeons (right) live in the tropical areas of Africa and Asia. They are much more colorful than most northern pigeons.

coastal cliffs, as well as on small islands. The rock dove often nests in caves, sometimes in large colonies.

The Treroninae is another important subfamily of the Columbidae. These pigeons most often live in trees and eat fruit. One of the most characteristic genera is *Treron,* which includes many green pigeons found in Africa and Asia. Their basic color is a pastel green with various additions of yellow, orange, or mauve; even the beak and eyes may be brightly colored. The green pigeons have a strong gizzard designed to grind up the wild figs on which they feed.

Other species with brilliant coloration are members of the genera *Ptilinopus* and *Ducula* (the latter includes the Imperial pigeon). Most of these are found in the Indo-Malaysian area and in the Pacific, although a few species live in India. Two closely related pigeons, however, are found in Australia and New Zealand—the topknot pigeon, *Lopholaimus antarcticus,* and the New Zealand pigeon, *Hemiphaga novaeseelandiae.*

The islands of the Indian Ocean are the habitat of species belonging to the genus *Alectroenas* (the blue pigeon). Brown fruit-eating pigeons of the Philippines (genus *Phapitreon*) may also be members of this subfamily.

The Gourinae is a subfamily that includes the largest species of the entire family Columbidae. These are the crested pigeons of the genus *Goura*, which are indigenous to New Guinea. They are the size of large chickens. Their plumage is slate-blue with brick-red areas; they also have an elegant crest of rigid feathers.

The Didunculinae is a subfamily composed of a single species, the tooth-billed pigeon, *Didunculus strigirostris*, found only in Samoa.

The Dodo and the Solitaires were members of the family Raphidae. The three species of this family, which were close relatives of the Columbidae and resembled giant, flightless pigeons, are extinct.

The best-known species, the flightless dodo, *Raphus cucullatus*, was a bizarre bird. Larger than a turkey, it had a large head and an enormous beak that was hooked at the tip. It once flourished on the islands of Mauritius, Rodriguez, and Réunion in the Indian Ocean. When Europeans invaded the islands with domestic animals, the big birds were doomed, and they became extinct by the end of the 17th century. Previously isolated and safe from large predators, the dodo had lost the capacity to fly; its eggs and young fell victim to the pigs and rats that were imported by the settlers.

Cuckoos and Turacos—Cuculiformes

The order Cuculiformes includes a large number of unusual birds that range from the size of sparrows to the size of pheasants. Some species live in the trees, others on the ground. They are grouped in one order because of various anatomical similarities, including zygodactylous toes—two toes projecting forward and two backward. Other similarities include rather long bodies; large pointed or rounded wings; and a relatively long tail with eight to ten stabilizing feathers. The bill is slender and curves slightly downward at the tip. The plumage is usually a dull brown, gray, or black, but tropical species may be brilliantly plumed and colored.

Birds of this order have a rather furtive nature and are more apt to be heard than seen. Some are parasitic—they let birds of another species incubate and hatch their eggs, and birds of still another species take responsibility for their young. Many cuculiforms choose a communal life, in which several pairs of birds share the responsibilities of incubating the eggs and caring for the young. Members of this order are found in all parts of the world, except in the very cold regions where there are few insects.

The Cuckoos belong to the family Cuculidae. They have a bad reputation as parasites because some leave their eggs for other birds to incubate and hatch. Actually, not all cuckoos are guilty of this behavior. Some build their own nests and care for their young.

The way in which the parasitic cuckoos impose their young on other birds is both clever and interesting. The parents don't drop their eggs at random; they carefully select the host. One of the main criteria is the host's diet: grain-eaters are bypassed in favor of insect-eaters because young cuckoos prefer the insect diet characteristic of their family. Fortunately for the parents, they can select among a wide range of species.

Parasitic cuckoos tend to be very particular. For example, one cuckoo will always choose the nests of meadow pipits while another selects those of meadow warblers. Often the eggs of the trespasser resemble those of the host, which provides a protective camouflage. In some cases, this resemblance extends even to young, especially when the hosts are permitted by the cuckoo nestlings to raise their own brood. An example is the

A peaceful dove Geopelia striata *(near right) takes a sunbath. "Dove" is a general term for smaller species of the pigeon family; "pigeon" is used for larger species.*

The dodo (far right) became extinct in the 17th century. It could not fly, and its eggs and young became easy prey for pigs, rats, and man.

This delicately colored stock dove was once plentiful in Europe, but hunters have sharply reduced its numbers. It prefers the woods, but can also make its home in the fields and even on barren land. Often it nests in the hollow of a tree, among rocks or even in a rabbit's den. One place its nest will never be found, however, is in the branches of trees.

koel cuckoo, *Eudynamys scolopaceus*, of southern Asia, which deposits its eggs in the nests of birds such as the raven. The cuckoo nestlings are as coal black as the raven, even though their true mother is brown with white spots.

Often, the hosts are not permitted to raise their own young because the aggressive cuckoo nestlings eject their rivals from the nest. The young cuckoos' intelligence is clearly inherited from the true parents, who carefully drop their eggs into the chosen nest while the hosts are away.

The parasitic cuckoos of the subfamily Cuculinae are numerous and are found throughout the Old World, Australia and New Zealand, but most of the species inhabit the tropical zones of Africa.

The Anis of the subfamily Crotophaginae are among the most interesting of the non-parasitic cuckoos. The ani solves its home-making problem by building large communal nests in which a number of females deposit their eggs. These appear to be hatched by the entire community, with each member taking its turn sitting on the eggs. There are four species—three in the genus *Crotophaga* and one in the genus *Guira*.

The Phaenicophaeinae are a subfamily of non-parasitic nest-builders. However, their nests are somewhat haphazard, and the hens sometimes absentmindedly drop their eggs in the nests of other birds.

This group is found in Africa, America, and the Orient. Eight genera are distributed

The greater roadrunner (right) can fly, but it prefers the ground to the air. It has typical cuculiform feet: two toes in front and two behind. But this does not keep it from being a very speedy runner and catching swift lizards.

in Asia from Ceylon to the Philippines; three genera are American—*Coccyzus, Piaya,* and *Saurothera.* The two species (*C. eythrophthalamus* and *C. americanus*) that nest in the United States and Canada feed on hairy caterpillars. They are highly migratory.

Running Cuckoos of the subfamily Neomorphinae are found mostly in the New World —the southwestern part of the United States, Mexico, and Central America. Several species are nest-builders, establishing their own nests and caring for the young.

The roadrunner, *Geococcyx californianus,* is the best-known species of this subfamily. A handsome and courageous bird, it aggressively confronts snakes and lizards, which are the staples of its diet. It has black stripes,

a head crest, and rather long legs, well-adapted for running.

The Coucal of the subfamily Centropodinae is another bird with curious nesting habits. It builds its nest in tall grass and enters the globular structure through a tunnel. The female lays 3 to 5 eggs, which usually do not hatch at the same time because the mother sits on each egg as she lays it. This bird is found from Africa to Australia.

Cuckoos often leave their eggs for other birds to incubate and hatch. A young Eurasian cuckoo (left) waits to be fed by its foster parents.

The female koel (above) represents another species of Old World parasitic cuckoo. The males of this species are all black.

59

The Couas of the subfamily Couinae are found in Madagascar. There are 10 species in this little-known group. They are generally terrestrial forest birds that build their own nests and care for their own young. They feed on fruit and insects.

The Turacos, or **Plantain-eaters,** of the family Musophagidae are found only in Africa. These birds live and run about in the branches of trees. They are about the size of pigeons and have short, rounded wings that restrict them to brief flights. Two genera, *Turacus* and *Musophaga*, include species whose special red and green pigments make them unique in the bird world. They are among the most brilliantly colored birds in all of Africa.

In most birds, the color green results from a combination of two or more pigments. In turacos, however, green is produced by a single substance called turacoverdin. The true nature of turacoverdin is not fully understood, but it is found only in the plumage of the turacos. The beautiful red of the wings and head feathers, which is also unique, is due to the presence of turacin, a water-soluble copper compound.

Aside from the extraordinary brilliance of their plumage, little is known about the turacos. It is almost impossible to conduct scientific observations of them as they scramble through the trees. They have not yet been able to reproduce in captivity, although their appetites are good and they devour fruit just as avidly as they do in their wild state.

The Musophagidae build simple, rather crude nests, and normally lay two eggs that hatch after about 20 days of brooding. The nestlings are born with thick down and claws so well-developed that they can easily wander around the branches of their home tree or nearby trees long before they are ready to fly. Both parents supply food, which consists of partially digested fruit pulp.

The various species are divided into five genera. Only one species, the giant turaco, *Corythaeola cristata*, reaches a large size. Other genera are *Crinifer*, with two species; *Corythaixoides*, with three; *Musophaga*, with two; and *Turacus*, with ten. Most species have a subdued coloring, running to grays and browns. The more flamboyantly colored birds have not only reds and greens but blue and violet tints in their plumage as well. The giant turaco, for instance, has a green and blue plumage with no red at all.

Almost all turacos are crested with red or white-tipped feathers. The head-covering resembles hair more than feathers because the individual plumes have few or no lateral shafts. Two other distinctive features are the strong, short, curved beak, and the peculiarly shaped and positioned nostrils.

Certain of the turacos have a wide distribution in Africa. These include the giant turaco and Ross's plantain-eater, *Musophaga rossae*. This latter species prefers the tropical forests of the central strip of Africa, which stretches from the Congo to Angola and Uganda. The dry savannah that extends south of the tropical rain forests is the home of the gray turaco, *Corythaixoides concolor*.

The turacos are a subject of dispute among ornithologists because some species show a resemblance to the South American hoatzin, suggesting that they may be related to that species. However, the composition of their eggs and many of their external features suggest that they belong to the cuckoo order.

Nocturnal Birds of Prey— Strigiformes

The owls, which are night-flying birds of prey, make up the order Strigiformes. They have some unusual features that enable them to hunt very efficiently at night. The huge eyes have great light-gathering power, and the ears are so keenly attuned to the slightest rustling in the woods that some owls can detect a mouse in total darkness.

All owls have short tails and large heads. The large eyes are set in the front of the head and encircled with feathery discs. The beak is hooked and partially hidden by the facial disc feathers. The feet are very efficient weapons, due to an outer toe that may be turned forward, backward or sideways; when the owl attacks its prey, the toe is turned back. The claws are curved and sharp.

Owls are able to blend easily into the background because the color of their plumage differs according to habitat. Those living in woods are mostly brown and gray, with streaks, mottles, and bars looking like the bark of trees. The snowy owl, *Nyctea seandiaca*, is white with black markings, making it inconspicuous in the low vegetation and rocks of its native Arctic, where the terrain is nearly always partially covered with snow. Many species of owls have a melodious call; others produce whistling, or even baying notes.

The owl's wings are so constructed that it can swoop down on its prey in silence. This remarkable silence is achieved by the unique wing feathers. These are fringed with filaments that break the air into tiny streams, thus making little noise. Owls that hunt fish do not have need of this particular characteristic since underwater prey cannot hear flight noise.

All owls have large eyes, which are often yellow. They are equipped with a thickened cornea that serves as a magnifying lens. The many light-sensitive retinal cells register the faintest light rays and contribute to the owl's ability to hunt at night. However, despite the popular belief that owls cannot see during the day, experiments have proven the contrary. Certain species, such as the hawk owl and the snowy owl, hunt regularly in daytime.

Owls have large ear openings that facilitate keen sound perception. The importance of hearing in their night hunting has been shown in experiments on the common barn owl. When the ears are blocked, the bird is unable to swoop down on its prey with its usual accuracy.

Most owls live in trees, in a wide variety of environments. Virtually all feed on animals; their prey includes insects, worms, crabs, amphibians, snakes, birds, and certain small mammals. Rodents are especially common prey. Members of the African genus *Scotopelia* and the Asian genus *Keputa* feed on fish.

Rather than build nests, most owls deposit their eggs in holes in trees, the abandoned nests of other species, or in other abandoned structures. The incubation period can last from 27 to 36 days, depending on the species. The nestlings are born with their eyes and ears closed. They are covered with a white down, which is soon replaced by a thick down that is sometimes marked with stripes. This, in turn, is replaced by the plumage of the adolescent birds, which closely resembles the true adult plumage.

Most owls are sedentary. Some species, however, such as the Eurasian scops owl, regularly leave the cold continent to winter in the warm weather of the Mediterranean islands or the African coast.

Owls can be found in all countries and in most environments. While the order is fairly homogenous, it is divided into two families, the Tytonidae, with about ten species, all barn owls, and the Strigidae, with at least 120 species.

The burrowing owl (opposite page) lives in prairies. Often it nests in the deserted burrows of prairie dogs. It ducks into the burrow when danger threatens.

The Barn Owls have fared better than other owls in their adaptation to humans. They readily take up residence in stables, belfries, or ruins, where they prey on mice, their favorite food. The features that set them apart from the rest of the owls include their long thin legs, proportionately smaller eyes, and facial disc feathers, which are heart-shaped rather than circular. The best-known species is the common barn owl, *Tyto alba*, which is found throughout most of the world.

The Family Strigidae includes all owls except barn owls. There are more than 120 species grouped into 25 genera. Many of the species are hunted by man because of the mistaken notion that they are harmful to small game. As a result, some species have become quite rare, and the laughing owl, *Sceloglaux albifacies*, of New Zealand is extinct.

In many species of this family the heads bear tufts of feathers shaped like ears or horns. The tufts break up the outline of the bird and make it less visible.

The giants of the family are the eagle owls of the genus *Bubo*. These birds are found in Europe, Asia, and parts of Africa and America. The great horned owl, *Bubo virginianus*, lives in America. A magnificent bird, it is 2 feet long and has prominent ear tufts 2 inches long. The two smallest owls, the elf owl, *Micrathene whitneyi*, and the pygmy owl, *Glaucidium gnoma*, are both found in the western United States. The saw-whet, or Acadian owl, *Aegolius acadius*, is about 8 inches long; it is the smallest owl indigenous to the eastern United States.

The commonest owl in North America is the screech owl, *Otus asio*. Not much larger than the robin, though considerably heavier, its call is not really a screech but a low tremulous whistle.

Goatsuckers— Caprimulgiformes

The common name, goatsuckers, for the members of the order Caprimulgiformes came from man's erroneous belief that these birds suck goats' milk. The Latin *capri mulgus* means "milker of goats," and evidence shows that this belief was engrained in men's minds even during the time of the ancient Greeks.

The downy young are in the center of this family of barn owls (near right). At one time barn owls nested in hollow trees, but now they seem to prefer belfries and towers.

The saw-whet owl (far right) is no bigger than a sparrow. Its name describes its rasping cry, which sounds like sharpening, or whetting, a saw.

Goatsuckers actually feed on insects, which they catch in flight—the birds use their gaping beaks to scoop up the passing insects. The goatsucker's trilling call has inspired the name "nightjar," because their call "jars" the night. This order includes birds called frogmouths, oilbirds, potoos, nighthawks, and whippoorwills. The last two are the most common goatsuckers in North America.

There are five families in the order Caprimulgiformes. They are characterized by a large, slightly flattened head; large eyes that are well-adapted to nocturnal life; and a beak that looks small when closed but is impressively wide when opened. Their wings vary in size and shape, and most are good flyers. Their legs are so short and weak that when these birds are at rest, they appear to

be legless. The dull coloring of the plumage —a pattern of black-and-white markings on a gray or brown background—provides an excellent camouflage.

The Nightjars of the family Caprimulgidae include about 70 species grouped into 18 genera. They are distributed throughout the world. The species are all similar in appearance, invariably having a weak, small beak. The beak is surrounded by stiff sensitive hairs that enable the nightjar to capture insects at night. The tail is long, and the quills on the males of some species are peculiarly shaped. The protective coloration of the nightjars is particularly effective.

The Nighthawks of the subfamily Chordeilinae are found only in the New World. They

Five species of owls are grouped on these two pages.

The snowy owl (below left) lives in arctic regions.

The eagle owl (below right), one of the giants of the family, is related to the American great horned owl.

A little owl (opposite page, top left) and a young scops owl (opposite page, top right) are both found in Europe.

A young milky owl (opposite page, bottom), found in Africa, is one of the largest members of the family.

differ from other goatsuckers in that they lack the stiff hairs at the sides of the mouth. Common nighthawks, *Chordeiles minor,* can be found during the summer from Florida to Alaska, but in winter they migrate to South America. They are gargantuan eaters, likely to consume as many as 1,800 flying ants or 500 mosquitoes a day. They can sometimes be seen at dusk, often in cities where they nest on flat gravel roofs.

The European Nightjar and the **North American Whippoorwill** belong to the subfamily Caprimulginae. Although the nightjar may nest in Europe, northern Africa or Asia, it migrates as far south as South Africa for the winter. The feathers of Caprimulginae give these birds a false appearance of large size. The plumage is mottled brown.

The North American whippoorwill, which is approximately 10 inches in length, is named for its distinctive call. Repeated frequently, this shrill phrase has disturbed the sleep of many a camper in mountain woodlands. The bird is known, too, to many only through its call, rather than its appearance. Not only is the whippoorwill nocturnal but also it is exceedingly well camouflaged. Even during the day, should it be resting on dead leaves, the bird is virtually invisible. The whippoorwill nests on the ground, in well-drained land. It doesn't bother to construct a nest, using merely a slight depression in dead leaves.

The Owlet-frogmouths belong to the small family Aegothelidae. The eight species of this group are tree-dwelling goatsuckers that inhabit a wide area from New Guinea to Australia. Five species live in New Guinea, two are common to Indonesia and New Caledonia, and one is found in Australia.

Like owls, they stand erect. They are about 10 inches long. They differ from the nightjars in the placement of eggs and in the appearance of the nestlings. Species of the genus *Aegotheles* deposit their white eggs in the hollows of trees or in holes in sandbanks, while the nightjars lay them in the underbrush or in dry vegetation. The nestling of the owlet-frogmouth is born with a white covering of down, while the nightjars grow a grayish down after birth.

The Potoos of the family Nyctibiidae are found in Central and South America. The mouth of these goatsuckers, which is bright orange inside, is large enough to close over a tennis ball. These birds live in forests that are not dense, but they nevertheless manage to camouflage themselves.

Their nesting habits consist of laying one egg on top of a broken snag. The hen broods over it in an erect position, becoming completely immobile and rigid at the sign

of danger. These species hunt only at night, flying out from the tree branches to seize insects.

One species, the common potoo, *Nyctibius griseus,* has a hauntingly beautiful night song. This bird, which is plumed in a variety of gray shades, seems to call, in lamentation, "poor-me-one." The potoos, like many of their relatives, are seldom seen. But their melancholy cries have fascinated many of the Indians in their range. Some Indians consider the potoo's wails omens of calamity.

The True Frogmouths of the family Podargidae include a dozen species that live in tree branches in the Oriental and Australian tropics. Three species of the genus *Podargus* are native to Australia, New Guinea, and the Solomon Islands, while the nine species of the genus *Batrachostomus* are distributed from India to Malaysia.

The frogmouths are also known as cavemouths. The large mouth led naturalists to believe that these birds were excellent trappers of flying insects. However, closer obser-

vation has disproved this theory—they are quite sluggish and limit themselves to feeding on larger insects that hop on branches or the ground. Some species also eat small mammals, birds, and fruit. Although they are not strong flyers, the true frogmouths are capable of rapid, short-distance flights. Both genera construct tiny lichen-covered nests.

The Guacharo, *Steatornis caripensis,* is the only member of the family Steatornithidae. Also known as the oil-bird, it is also the only vegetarian in an insect-eating order. It feeds primarily on the oily fruits of palm trees as well as on aromatic and succulent fruits of other tropical trees. Like other goatsuckers the guacharo has a strong, curved beak surrounded by stiff hairs. Its wingspread measures up to 36 inches.

The guacharo lives in the Caribbean islands and in South America, where is spends its day in caves hidden in the forests, coming out only at night to feed. Huge flocks leave their nests at twilight, and their sharp

cries echo through the forest. They pluck the fruit while hovering above the branches. These flocks travel as many as 50 miles in search of ripe fruit and return the same night. Oil-birds are trapped locally, since their body grease makes excellent lamp oil and a butter substitute.

Inside their caves, they build nests made of a paste consisting of partially digested and regurgitated fruit. Two or four eggs are laid within an interval of a few days and are brooded for more than a month. Nestlings remain with the parents for several months, and are well-developed by the time they leave the nest.

Europeans first heard of the guacharo in 1799, when a German explorer, Alexander von Humboldt, visited some caves in Venezuela. There he captured a few specimens, and noted the intense noise made by the large bird population. In 1953, an American professor named Donald Griffin showed that these cries are a kind of sonar system that enables the bird to find its way around in the total darkness of the caves.

Swifts and Hummingbirds— Apodiformes

The hummingbirds and swifts of the order Apodiformes seem very different from each other. Yet they are placed in the same order because they share a number of internal structural similarities. Both spend most of their time in the air. Consequently, they have tremendous pectoral, or flight, muscles in relation to their size. Their legs are very short, but they have sharp claws that enable them to cling to perches.

The Swifts of the family Apodidae are fast flyers. Their speeds range from 60 to possibly 150 miles per hour. The fastest flyers are the larger swifts of Asia and the Middle East. Swifts are able to drink, catch insects, bathe, and sleep while in flight. In fact, they can even mate in the air, a unique practice among birds. The only activity that does not occur in flight is nesting.

Gaucharos, or oilbirds (center), build their nests deep inside caves. Here they live in darkness, communicating through short cries that act as a kind of sonar system as the sound waves bounce off the cave walls.

The nightjar (above) is a good example of mimetic coloring—coloring that serves as camouflage. When it freezes and closes its eyes, it is almost invisible as it roosts by day, lengthwise on a branch.

A hummingbird approaches a flower. It will suck the nectar and pick up any small insects that may be there.

There are about 100 species of swifts. All have small, ellipsoidal bodies, large heads that barely project from the body, and large, flat beaks with stiff hairs at the base. They have a sooty black coloring, with some white or gray areas on the throat, breast, and back.

Swifts have a unique method of nest-building: all species use a special paste made from the secretion of the salivary glands to glue the various materials together. The nests of the chimney swifts consist of a little platform of twigs stuck together and attached to a wall or the inside of a chimney with the salivary glue. Before the advent of chimneys, these swifts built their nests in hollow trees. The chimney sweeps of North America are members of the subfamily Chaeturineae. Their tail feathers have spiny tips that help them cling to vertical walls.

The swallow-tailed swift (*Panyptila*) of tropical America constructs feltlike tubes, which it hides beneath rocky shelves. The Afro-Asian palm swift, *Cypsiurus parvas*, simply glues two eggs to a feltlike pad that it has attached to palm leaves.

A group of about 20 species of small swifts belonging to the genus *Collocalia* nest in caves in southeast Asia and on the islands of the Indian and Pacific Oceans. They build moon-shaped nests that in a few species are made entirely of saliva. The bird's-nest soup of Chinese restaurants uses the nests of these swifts.

Nine species living in tropical America belong to the genus *Cypseloides*.

The subfamily Apodinae includes five genera, of which the best-known is *Apus*. This genus includes the Eurasian swift, *A. apus*, the pallid swift, *A. pallidus*, and the Alpine swift, *A. melba* of the Mediterranean region. Most of the *Apus* species are African in origin.

The common Eurasian swift is among the most familiar of these birds. It has the interesting characteristic of relating its nesting habits to its food supply. If the food supply

is adequate, the bird lays two eggs at two-day intervals; in times of famine, the interval is three days. Although the parents generally share brooding, they leave the eggs untended if food is scarce. The eggs are resistant to low temperatures. The nestlings are hardy creatures and can be left without food for long periods. This allows the parents to make extended trips lasting several days in their search for food.

The Crested Swifts of the family Hemiprocnidae are found from India to the Solomon Islands. The four species of crested swifts are the only swifts that can perch on wires

The calliope hummingbird (above) is a species native to the western United States and Canada. Its brilliant throat is visible only in direct light.

and tree branches. The nest, which holds only one egg, is built on the branch of a tree.

The crested swifts of the genus *Hemiprocne* build fragile nests of bark, down, and glue just large enough to hold one egg; another species makes a moss nest and affixes it behind a waterfall.

The crested tree swift, *H. mystacea*, is distributed through Malaysia and Australia. It is a basically black bird, with rather long white whiskers at the side of the head. Like other members of the family, it has an erectile crest and a deeply forked tail.

The Hummingbirds are members of the family Trochilidae. Although certain swifts are among the fastest flyers in the bird world, the hummingbird is singular in its ability to hover in the air. The only bird that can back away in flight when faced with danger, the hummingbird cannot actually fly backwards, as is popularly believed. With a brisk downward scoop of the tail, it can reverse its wings, which are mounted as on a swivel, and move back before making an escape.

Hummingbirds have many remarkable features. One species, the Cuban bee hummingbird, *Calypte helenae,* is only 2 inches long. It is the smallest bird—and the smallest higher vertebrate—in the world. Other hummingbird species measure as long as 9 inches. The sword-beaked hummingbird, *Ensifera ensifera,* is the only bird in which the bill is as long as the body. Both measure over 8 inches.

The wing structure of the hummingbird is most unusual. The wings are long, but the upper arm bone is very short. Thus the wing extends out from the shoulder, almost like a hand. The average wing beat rate is an astonishing 50 to 70 beats per second. This rate, however, can reach 80 beats per second in the violet hummingbird, *Calliphlox amethystina*. By comparison, a pigeon can beat its wings only 5 to 8 times per second.

A hummingbird in flight (right) is caught by a high speed camera lens. Its wings flap so fast that they must be photographed at 1/5,000 of a second.

Hummingbirds of all species live on insects and the nectar of flowers; their bills are shaped so that they can extract the nectar. The hummingbird's brilliant coloring is perhaps its most remarkable feature. The rainbow hues are a result of the most simple types of pigment, black and red, contained

in the feathers of birds. The secret of the brilliant hues lies in the structure of the hummingbird's feathers, which deflect light rays, breaking them into bands of the colors of the spectrum. In certain lights, however, the colors do not reflect, and the birds appear quite dull. As a rule, males and females have noticeably different coloring and ornamental tufts of feathers. Members of the genera *Stephanoxis* and *Lophornis* have handsome crests; both males and females of *Phaethornis* have subdued plumage.

Usually, the only sound of a hummingbird is the humming produced by the wings. However, in the mating season the male makes excited chirping sounds.

The appetite of these birds is proportionate to the energy spent in their frenetic activities; their dizzying flight dehydrates them,

Since they are daytime birds, hummingbirds stop feeding at dusk and may fall into a state of inertia, which conserves their energy at night. This inertia may be related to the lower temperatures at night. In experiments, birds warmed by lamp heat always revive quickly.

The ruby-throated hummingbird is the only hummer found in the eastern part of the United States and Canada. This tiny bird arrives in its northern habitat in late spring, after a flight that sometimes includes a 500-mile trip across the Gulf of Mexico.

forcing them to drink often. Hummingbirds feed constantly in order to maintain their exhausting pace. They eat not only the nectar of flowers but also spiders and small, soft-bodied insects, which they catch in flight. They drink without coming to rest, collecting dew and rain water from leaves and flowers or from holes in the trunks and branches of trees. These birds can often be seen flying close to waterfalls. The advantage of this aerial maneuvering is that the falls moisten the birds with spray.

Hummingbirds have to be very mobile in order to provide themselves with the large amounts of food they need. For example, hummingbirds in the western part of the United States migrate to the Pacific Ocean coastal lands in early spring when the flowers are in bloom. In late summer, they fly up to mountain meadows.

The hummingbird's reproductive habits are only partially known to man, principally because it is difficult to observe birds that move so quickly. Males of some species

Lovebirds are small parrots, named for their habit of cuddling side-by-side on a perch. Often a couple will sit and chatter to each other for hours. Quite small, they do not exceed 7 inches in length. Their plumage is generally green, but facial coloring varies from species to species. Shown here is the Abyssinian lovebird Agapornis taranta.

gather in arenas where they perform aerial dances or engage in struggles for supremacy. Except for the short courting and mating period, the sexes generally live apart, each defending its own territory. All responsibilities for nesting fall on the female.

The nests are intricately constructed of plant-down or catkins, and the outside resembles the knot of a tree. The female deposits two eggs which, after a variable period of incubation, produce featherless nestlings with closed eyes. The young grow feathers very soon, without passing through a downy stage; they remain in the nest for about three weeks.

Hummingbirds, though tiny, have an aggressive temperament and do not hesitate to attack animals much larger than themselves, including man, by diving at the enemies with incredible speed.

In general structure, all species are similar. The keel of the sternum, or breastbone, is very deep and long, and allows space for the powerful flight muscles. Like those of the swift, the hummingbird's legs are very short and have four toes with small sharp claws. The beak varies among genera both in shape and length. The shape of the wing varies little among species. It has ten flight feathers, while the tail has ten guide feathers. The guide feathers can be almost any size or shape from square to forked, from triangular to rounded.

Hummingbirds are found only in North and South America. Attempts to introduce them to Europe have never been successful. They probably originated in the Andes Mountains of South America, in Colombia or Ecuador, where the majority of species are still found. They are distributed as far south as Patagonia and as far north as Alaska.

Most species stay close to home and to each other. Of the 18 species in the United States, only the ruby-throated hummingbird lives east of the Mississippi River. It migrates nonstop across the Gulf of Mexico.

Parrots—Psittaciformes

The parrots of the order Psittaciformes are probably best known for their imitations of the human voice and for their gaudy plumage. An interesting little fact is that parrots are generous about sharing their food with other parrots. Throughout the world's tropical forests, shrieking flocks, flying above the dense foliage, receive an answering shriek of invitation from a hidden flock that has found a scarce tree with ripening fruit.

Parrots form a very homogeneous group, and there is only one family in the order.

From the strip of tropical forests that circle the earth, parrots have spread to the

The red-faced lovebirds (below) are a species of the genus Agapornis. These birds make their nest in a hole with shreds of leaf or grass.

south and even to colder areas northward. The biggest concentration of these birds remains in Australia and the Amazon River basin in South America.

All have a rounded head, a short neck, and strong wings, which permit the smaller species to fly "like bullets" while the larger species often fly long distances to find food. One species, the hairy-faced owl parrot, or kakapo, is completely flightless. It forages for leaves, young shoots, berries, and moss in the forests of New Zealand. Most parrots spend their days creeping about the high branches of trees, flying only to go on foraging expeditions.

The sulfur-crested cockatoo (below) is named for its sulfur-yellow crest. The white plumage is typical of cockatoos.

Their legs are generally short, with two toes in front and two in the rear. Their feet provide a remarkable degree of dexterity,

and they climb trees readily, often using their beaks as a third "hand."

The parrots' brightly colored plumage is most frequently green, but some are scarlet, and others are entirely blue. With few exceptions, they nest in the hollows of trees. Certain species dig into termite mounds to hollow nesting chambers. The monk parrot of Argentina lives communally in tall, multi-chambered dwellings made of twigs.

Depending upon the species, two to eight eggs are deposited in a bare cavity or on a bed of dry leaves. African lovebirds of the genus *Agapornis* thrust grass and bits of leaves between the feathers of the back and breast in order to carry them to their nests.

The young, which are born without down, are fed partially digested food that is regurgitated by their parents. Eating habits vary considerably among the parrots of the Australian region. The galah cockatoo digs for roots with its beak, while other species dig for grubs in the soil or sip nectar somewhat like the hummingbird. Most species, however, feed on fruits and seeds.

The order Psittaciformes has about 315 species, divided into some 82 genera. The one family, Psittacidae, is divided into 6 subfamilies.

The Subfamily Nestorinae includes two species that have been known to kill sheep, tearing out the meat and fat with their beaks. Originally these birds were seed and fruit eaters, and the exact reason for this curious change in diet is unknown. It has been suggested that the Nestorinae first tasted flesh by accident while searching through sheeps' wool for parasites.

These birds include the kea, *Nestor notabilis*, and the kaka, *N. meridionalis*. Natives of New Zealand and its neighboring islands, they both have a rather compressed beak and dark-brown or olive coloration. The kaka is about 20 inches long, including an 8-inch

tail, while the kea is somewhat larger and has a thinner beak.

The Owl Parrot, *Strigops habroptilus*, is the only member of the subfamily Strigopinae. Like its namesake the owl, this parrot has a circle of facial disc-feathers. Unable to fly, the bird has short wings. Found in New Zealand, this charming and unique parrot is almost extinct.

The Lories of the subfamily Loriinae have brilliant coloring and a small beak. The brushlike tip of the tongue enables them to collect pollen and nectar from many flowers, especially those of the eucalyptus tree. They also eat fruits and insects. Members of this subfamily are distributed throughout Australasia and surrounding regions.

The True Parrots of the subfamily Psittacinae include the love-birds, parakeets, and macaws, as well as a number of unusual birds.

Like the bat, the bat parrot hangs upside down from tree branches. The wavy parrot is a common pet, as is the talking gray parrot of Africa. The Andean parakeets of the genus *Bolbarhynchus* thrive on thin air.

The Dwarf Parrots of the subfamily Micropsittinae are the smallest birds of the parrot order. They measure only 4½ inches in length. Forest-dwellers, they have a varied diet consisting of fruits, fungi, and insects. Both male and female have short tails but the male is darker. These birds are species of the genus *Micropsitta*.

The Cockatoos of the subfamily Cacatuinae are distinguished from other parrots by an erectile crest. The palm cockatoo, *Probosciger aterrimus*, and the black cockatoos of the genus *Calyptorhynchus* are dark, but most members of this subfamily are very light, even white. Their bills are powerful and well adapted to their diet of nuts and hard fruits. They are found in Australia, New Guinea, and the Indonesian islands.

The kea (above left) lives high in the New Zealand Alps. It is one of the few parrot species to inhabit a cold region.

The rainbow lorikeets (above right), of the Australian region, have very bright plumage. Their tongue ends in a brush-tip that serves for sucking nectar and pollen from flowers.

Three members of the
subfamily Psittacinae, the
"true" parrots, are the
scarlet macaw (opposite
page), the African gray
parrot (top left), and
the Amazon (bottom). The
African gray and the
Amazon are favorite cage
species.

The huge palm cockatoo
(top right) is a member
of the subfamily Kaka-
toeniae. It lives in North
Australia and New
Guinea.

Mousebirds—Coliiformes

The mousebirds of the small order Coliiformes slightly resemble mice both in appearance and behavior. They are found only in Africa. These birds have been grouped into one family, the Coliidae, primarily on the basis of their foot structure, which includes heavy, hooked claws and an outer toe that pivots in a forward and backward motion. This foot enables the bird to scamper along tree branches in a mouselike fashion. The plumage, grayish feathers that resemble hair, adds to the bird's mouselike qualities. The head has a plumed crest.

The mousebird is quite small, usually no larger than the sparrow, but with a long tail.

It flies gracefully and moves in a weaving fashion. At night, mousebirds gather in small groups in the shelter of a large bush or tree. And, probably for mutual support, they fall asleep leaning against one another, forming columns along the branches. Their diet consists primarily of fruits, although they do feed on some vegetables. Recently the Kenya white-cheeked mousebird, or coly, was observed feeding on insects, although fruit is its mainstay. Mousebirds are often considered vermin by African farmers because the birds devastate orchards.

Depending on the species, the mousebird's nest may be in a hole or it may be a cup covered with grass. There are two to four eggs, sometimes spotted in different shades.

The redfaced mousebird (below left) has red rings around its eyes. Sometimes, this bird hangs upside down on a branch.

Occasionally a mousebird comes to the ground (below right). This bird is named for its grayish coloring and scampering movements.

Trogons—Trogoniformes

The trogons of the order Trogoniformes are among the most beautiful birds in the world. They are grouped in one family, the Trogonidae, which includes some 35 species in 8 genera.

The family is known to be an ancient one because fossil remains found in Europe date back to the Upper Eocene, about 40 million years ago. Today, most trogons live in Central and South America, where there are some 20 species. In Africa there are only 3 species; there are 11 in Asia, from India to China and from Indonesia to the Philippines. Despite their concentration in the tropics, they are also found in cool, high areas.

Trogons may be up to 14 inches in length. The wings are short and rounded, and there is a long tail. The beak is short, thick, and curved at the edge. Their toes are unique among birds, with the first and second turning backward.

In some species, in the mating season, males make a series of vibrant, gutteral sounds. All trogons nest in the hollows of trees or in other holes. The average number of eggs is two or three. The parents share the task of incubating the eggs and caring for the helpless nestlings.

The male trogon generally has varied shades of red, orange, or yellow on its breast and belly, which contrast sharply with the colors of the throat and neck. The tail is

Speckled mousebirds, seen here eating their way through some fruit, are among the better known members of the order Coliiformes. All mousebirds are found in Africa.

A bird of brilliantly hued
feathers, the narina is
found throughout Africa.
Its *vivid pinkish-red
stomach feathers* provide
a bright note against
the somber, dark green
forests.

82

square with a black-and-white design. Some are a striking green with the heads, breasts, and backs colored in bright reds and pinks. The females generally have a more subdued coloring. Trogons are typical tree-dwelling birds, and most species live on large insects and fruit.

The Quetzal of Central America is the most spectacular trogon in appearance. It is golden-green about the neck, head, back, and wings. Its most outstanding features are a long train of green feathers and a plumed crest. The feathers of the train are touched with white and scarlet. The quetzal is a striking sight when it slashes through the gloom of the tropical forests.

The ancient Mexicans found the quetzal so impressive that they made it a demigod. A combination of god and serpent, it became the god of the air, whom the Aztecs called Quetzalcoatl, the feathered serpent. Today the quetzal is the national symbol of Guatemala, and is considered a symbol of freedom there. It was selected because, according to legend, it cannot live in captivity. Some quetzals, however, do survive in zoos, which is fortunate, since they are becoming increasingly rare in their homeland. Long ago, the Aztecs killed them in order to use the plumage at religious ceremonies. Today, the quetzal is endangered because the forest lands, which provide its food, are gradually being destroyed.

Kingfishers and Their Relatives—Coraciiformes

The members of the order Coraciiformes at first seem almost completely unrelated. They include the kingfishers, hornbills, bee-eaters, hoopoes, todies, motmots, and rollers—none of which appear at all similar to the untrained eye. Ornithologists, however, have found an apparent link in their syndactyl

The pictures show a female (above) and male (below) quetzal. The tail of the quetzal is not made up of quill feathers. Rather, it is made up of small feathers that are an extension of the upper tail coverts.

feet, which means that the three front toes are joined for part of their length. Other immediately apparent similarities are the long tail, the presence of plume crests, and the shape of the beak, which is strong and reasonably straight, except in the hornbills and the hoopoes.

The nest is always placed in a natural hollow or a hole dug for that purpose. The eggs are generally white, and the young are born naked and helpless. After hatching the eggs, many species no longer concern themselves with keeping the nests clean. These soon become filled with food scraps and excrement, and exude a disagreeable odor. Perhaps because of these messy nesting habits and the musty odor exuded by the female's green gland, the hoopoe, whose flesh is edible, is among the forbidden foods of the Old Testament. The female's foul odor, however, keeps enemies at bay.

Almost all species are brightly colored in shades of blue, green, pinkish brown, scarlet, and yellow. Species with a more modest coloration compensate by possessing complex color patterns.

The birds of this order, however, are extremely varied, and some exhibit unusual behavior. Kingfishers, despite their name, do not always eat fish. A number of species eat insects, snails, frogs, and lizards. They can, however, spear fish skillfully in the water with their long, heavy beaks. The todies are tiny and chubby.

The motmots of the American tropics pluck the barbs of their own tail feathers, and the resulting tips resemble tennis rackets. The female of the bizarre hornbill family sheds her feathers so completely during the molting period that she is quite naked and unable to fly. She stays in a walled-up nest cavity for safety and relies on the male

The only widespread kingfisher in North America is the belted kingfisher. The male (near right) has a grayish band across its chest. The female (far right) has a chestnut-colored breast band.

for food. While in this nest, she can give the young constant attention and protection.

The Kingfishers of the family Alcedinidae have the widest distribution of any group in the order. Only 11 of the some 90 species are found on the American continents; most live in southeast Asia and the Pacific areas.

Common characteristics of kingfishers include compact bodies, short necks, and rather large heads. The long, straight, pointed beaks are flat in some species, narrow and laterally compressed in others. As a rule, the wings are short and rounded; the legs are always short and have the syndactyl feet of the Coraciiformes. The third and fourth toes are joined for almost their entire length, and the second and third are joined at the base.

Tails vary in size—in some species they are very long, the result of the development of the central tail feathers that often flare at the end. The feathers are brilliantly hued with metallic, or lacquer-like, reflections. Dominant colors include reds, greens, blues, and violets in various combinations, with occasional black or white spots. The legs and beak are generally red.

Kingfishers have an immediately identifiable stance, for their backs are hunched as the result of their short necks. They are solitary birds, and can sit motionless for long periods with their heads apparently sunk deep between their shoulders.

The kingfisher's nest is a simple hollow at the end of a tunnel dug in a tree, sandy bank, or termite mound. The pure white eggs number from two to seven. The young are born naked, except for an occasional covering of fine down. They remain safely in the nest, cared for by both parents, until they are ready to fly.

Kingfishers that feed on fish capture their prey by diving into the water from a tree or plunging after hovering, surfacing with the fish in their beaks. The common kingfisher lives on fish, but other species feed on insects.

The family Alcedinidae is divided into three subfamilies.

The subfamily Cerylinae contains two genera—*Ceryle* and *Chloroceryle*. The genus

Residents of tropical regions of two different continents are shown on this page.

The pied kingfisher (above left) is common in Africa south of the Sahara Desert.

The blue-crowned motmot (above right), related to the kingfisher, is considered to be one of the most beautiful of American tropical birds.

The largest and most unusual of the kingfishers is the Australian laughing kookaburra (near and far right). Also known as the "laughing jackass" for its braying laugh, it comes to the ground frequently. Among other foods, this bird eats reptiles. The kookaburra on the far right has just caught its dinner— a small snake.

Ceryle contains several species, including the pied kingfisher, *C. rudis,* an aggressive bird about 10 inches long, which lives in small groups and fishes in the shallow waters of Africa and southwest Asia. Another member of this genus is the giant kingfisher, *C. maxima.* Found in Africa, it measures almost 20 inches in length. This bird feeds exclusively on fish, diving clumsily into the water from a fixed position. The belted kingfisher, *C. alcyon,* of North America is marked across the chest by a band. In males the band is grayish, while in females it is chestnut-colored.

The genus *Chloroceryle* contains four species; they are found only in the New World. One species, the green kingfisher, *C. americanus,* ranges from southern Texas into Mexico and south to Argentina.

The subfamily Alcedininae contains the genus *Alcedo,* whose best-known member is the common kingfisher, *A. atthis.* This bird is found in Europe and as far east as Japan. Many beautiful tales are told about this kingfisher, which was known as halcyon to the ancient Greeks. It was believed that the bird built a nest of fish bones that floated on the ocean waters, and then brooded on its eggs for two weeks. During these "halcyon days," the god of the winds kept the waters calm and peaceful. The genus *Alcedo* also includes other Asian and African species.

Other members of this subfamily are a species found in Madagascar, *Ispidina madagascariensis,* and 10 species of the genus *Ceyx,* which occur in the Far East and Australia. Birds of these two genera feed on insects rather than fish.

The subfamily Daceloninae includes the kookaburra and other "hunting" species. Some are large enough to attack small mammals on the ground; many are quite pugnacious, even attacking other birds. Members of this subfamily are sometimes called tree kingfishers.

The kookaburra, or laughing jackass, *Dacelo gigas,* is found in Australasia. Largest of the kingfishers, its name is derived from its loud cackling laugh. This unusual bird has developed a taste for reptiles and rodents, and in some areas, such as Tasmania, farmers depend on it to curb these

Europe is the home of this brightly-feathered common kingfisher. For vivid beauty, it can only be compared to a hummingbird. It is no larger than a sparrow and feeds on minnows.

pests. The kookaburra, brown and grayish-white, is about 19 inches long. Other species of the genus *Dacelo* are found in New Guinea.

The Todies of the family Todidae live on the islands of the Caribbean Sea. There are five species, usually one per island. They live in the lowlands of Cuba, Jamaica, Haiti, and Puerto Rico. Another species inhabits the damp mountain forests of Haiti and is distinguished from the other Todidae by its slimmer beak.

The five species are remarkably similar in appearance—they are small birds, perhaps 4 inches long. The top parts are light green, the lower parts white, and the throat red. While their shape is reminiscent of the kingfishers, their beaks are less massive, and their tails are proportionately longer than those of the Alcedinidae.

Todies spend much of their time quietly perched on low branches, occasionally flying off to capture the tiny insects and small lizards on which they feed.

Like many Coraciiformes the todies dig their nests in sandbanks. A tunnel, barely an inch in diameter, leads to a more spacious incubation chamber containing two to four eggs. Initially white, the eggs are soon colored by the dirt on which they are laid.

The Motmots are members of the family Momotidae. They are a family of striking birds named after the sounds made by the common motmot, *Momotus momota*. Other species have a quite different vocal style. Some utter frightening guttural noises, while others have a high melodious song.

The motmot's most interesting feature is its tail, which assumes the shape of a tennis racket when the bird preens and thins it. The central tail feathers are much longer than the side feathers, and, in the area next to the tip, the barbs have little resistance and fall off easily. When the motmot perches, the peculiar form of the tail is emphasized by its wagging motions, and it would appear that the bird is trying to draw attention to its ornament.

One of the most beautiful American tropical birds, the motmot has a particularly delicate coloring—a mixture of green, olive, and russet. Some species have a blue head, as well as a black patch on the throat. The bird can be as long as 22 inches and has a rather slender profile; the beak, curved and broad, is at least as long as the head. Its toes are joined in the manner of the kingfishers'.

Nests are built in a tunnel in banks of sand or earth. Both male and female help in the construction, and they often begin to build the nest months before it is time to lay the eggs. Like many of the Coraciiformes, motmots do not clean their nests. The eggs hatch after a three-week incubation period.

The nestlings are born with their eyes closed and without down or feathers. As with the kingfisher, the young are cared for by both parents. A month later, when they are ready to leave the nest, their plumage is like that of their parents except that the long central feathers have not yet developed. The parents occasionally return to the nest, especially during the winter.

Members of the family Momotidae spend long periods of time perched on tree branches waiting for prey. Insects, spiders, and small lizards are the preferred diet. When it spies its prey, the motmot pounces, and carries the victim off to a roosting spot, smashing it on a branch before eating it.

The eight species of motmots are grouped into six genera, of which four—*Eumomota*,

A blue-crowned motmot can pass long periods of time perched on the branch of a tree, waiting for its dinner to pass by. Its stout bill easily dismembers the largest insects or small lizards.

Baryphthengus, Hylomanes, and *Asphata*—have just one species each; *Momotus* and *Electron* have two species each.

One of the most elegant species is the turquoise-browed motmot, *Eumomota superciliosa,* which is found from southern Mexico to Costa Rica. The largest species is the russet motmot, which lives in the vicinity of the Amazon River. In contrast, the dwarf motmot is about the size of a thrush and has a short tail that lacks the "racket" tips.

The Bee-eaters of the family Meropidae are found in Asia and Africa, and one species is native to Australia. Most of these birds are tropical; even the species found in the temperate zones migrate regularly to warmer regions. Some of the tropical species also migrate, probably due to a scarcity of food.

Their diet consists chiefly of insects, especially bees, wasps, and other Hymenoptera, which are captured in flight, sometimes from a vantage point such as a tree, bush, or telegraph wire. These birds' method of feeding seems to indicate that they are inhabitants of treetops, but they nest in the ground. Their profile is rather long, quite like the motmots. Also like motmots, the Meropidae have long, slightly curved beaks, syndactyl feet, and long tails. The tails are usually squared, but some have elongated central stabilizers. In one species the tail is forked.

Their plumage is usually brightly colored, and is similar in both sexes. Various tones of green predominate, usually with some yellow, light blue, burnt chestnut, and red. There are often markings of black and white.

European bee-eaters (right) are expert at catching bees and wasps, their favorite foods. They swoop gracefully through the air in pursuit of this prey.

genera. The genus with the largest number of species and the broadest distribution is *Merops*. It includes the Eurasian bee-eater, *M. apiaster*, which nests from the western Mediterranean (the Iberian peninsula and North Africa) to Kashmir and western Siberia, as well as in the tropical areas of Africa and India.

Another widely distributed species is the Indian bee-eater, *M. superciliosus*, which is found from North Africa to New Guinea, with subspecies in eastern Africa and Madagascar.

Africa is the home of the largest number of species. In the plains south of the Sahara, the traveler frequently encounters dense flocks of the scarlet or Nubian species, *M. nubicus*, which is entirely red except for a magnificent green head with black eyebrows. Its tail has extremely long central feathers.

The genus *Melittophagus* is composed of eight exclusively African species. The smallest is the lesser bee-eater, *M. pusillus*. Only 6 inches long, it lives along the Equator from Senegal to Ethiopia. Other African species include the white-necked bee-eater, *Merops albicollis*, the fork-tailed bee-eater, *Dicrocercus hirundineus*, and the black-headed bee-eater, *Bombylonax breweri*. The two species of genus *Nyctiornis* are found in southeast Asia.

The Madagascar Cuckoo Roller, *Leptosomus discolor*, is the only member of the family Leptosomatidae. Also known as the kirombo, the cuckoo roller is more than 16 inches long. It has a short, strong beak, a rather long tail, and very short legs. The outer toe may be turned backward, as is typical of the cuckoos and owls.

Coloration differs with sex. The male is gray, with iridescent patches around the nape of the neck; the female's lower parts are reddish, and her nape is marked with black and russet bars. These birds live in forests and other wooded areas, forming

Most species are communal, even during the nesting season, when as many as a thousand birds, occasionally of two species, may come together on a single sandbank. Like many Coraciiformes, the bee-eaters build a tunneled nest, frequently in a vertical wall. When required to tunnel in soil, bee-eaters try to place the hatching chamber somewhat higher than the entrance to the tunnel to prevent flooding by rain water. The eggs are always white, since camouflage is unnecessary. They number from two to five, and are hatched by both parents.

Bee-eaters range in size from 6 to 15 inches. They are docile in nature, which makes it possible to approach and observe them in the wild. There are 24 species in 7

Some species of bee-eaters are feathered in bright colors. The carmine, or Nubian, bee-eater (left) is one of the most brilliant. This species inhabits the vast plains south of the Sahara Desert. Occasionally these birds travel in dense flocks that look like red clouds.

small groups that often fly above the tree-tops, whistling at regular intervals.

The cuckoo roller generally feeds from the upper branches of trees. It hunts both insects and small reptiles, such as chameleons and tiny lizards. Like many cuckoos, they prefer the hairy caterpillar. They lay their eggs in the hollows of old trees, but many of their other habits are still unknown.

The Family Brachypteraciidae includes three genera with five species of Coraciiformes confined to the island of Madagascar. While they are sometimes included in the family Coraciidae (true rollers), the peculiar distribution and decidedly terrestrial habits of the Brachypteraciidae suggest that they should be treated as a separate family.

The hoopoe is the only species of the family Upupidae. One of the more elegant birds, it has a fancy crest and wings and tail of alternating black and white bars.

These birds are quite large, with strong beaks, big heads, and rather large legs—traits that point to terrestrial habits. The tail, which varies in length with the species, is graduated. Coloration varies within a pastel range, and the plumage is similar in both sexes. Reasonably assured birds, they like to hop or run on the ground before launching into their short flights. Their call is not very loud, although the island inhabitants claim that these birds make terrifying sounds at night. Their diet is predominantly meat, consisting of insects, reptiles, and amphibians captured on land. While direct observations by scientists have been few, according to the local population, these rollers lay their eggs in holes that they dig in the earth.

The short-legged cuckoo roller, *Brachyp-*

teracias leptosomus, has beautiful blue shadings on the nape and back. The scaly ground roller, *B. squamigera,* has bright green feathers with dark edges that resemble scales.

The True Rollers belong to the family Coraciidae. One of the best-known members of this group is the common Eurasian roller, *Coracias garrulus.* It gets its name from aerial maneuvers performed during courting, when it seems to be "rolling" in the air. Actually, rolling is only one feat in a spectacular acrobatic repertory that includes dives, turns, banks, twists, and loops.

An inhabitant of Europe, Asia, and Africa, this roller, with its large head, powerful beak, blue plumage and russet back, is uninspiring when at rest. But when it takes flight, spreading its ultramarine, black bordered wings, it is indeed a magnificent sight.

Rollers are large birds, ranging from 10 to 14 inches. Despite their remarkable agility in flight, they are quite clumsy on the ground. The beak ends in a hook, and the legs are decidedly short and equipped with joined toes, as in other Coraciiformes.

The roller's keen eyes have a rather ferocious expression, and the bird is known to frighten passing birds of prey with an impressive display of dives and turns. The victim suffers no injury, but it does not readily attack the roller.

As a rule, the roller is solitary and will pass long hours perched on a branch, post, or telegraph wire, diving down from time to time to capture some insect or small vertebrate. When migrating, however, rollers sometimes form small groups. Generally found in migration along the coasts of the Mediterranean Sea, they are easily caught or killed by hunters.

The family includes a total of a dozen species in two genera, *Coracias* and *Eurystomus.* They are spread up and down the Eastern hemisphere, from southern Sweden to western Asia and Northern Africa. Those living in northern European areas migrate as far south as South Africa.

Coracias abyssinicus lives in Ethiopia and resembles the common Eurasian roller, but has longer outer-tail flight feathers. *Coracias cyanogaster,* another African species, has a blue belly, rose head, nape and breast, and a black beak. Its tail is preened into a tennis-racket webbing, as is that of the racket-tailed roller, *Coracias spatulatus,* which is also found in Africa. The genus *Coracias* includes two other African species and two from Asia.

Genus *Eurystomus* is composed of slightly smaller birds with beaks that are broader at the base than those of *Coracias.* Less talented in aerial acrobatics, two species of this genus are African, and one is found from India to Australia and the Solomon Islands. This

The Eurasian roller (left) is clumsy on the ground but extraordinarily agile in the air. It is the best-known member of the roller family.

Shown emerging from its
nest (right) is a broad-
billed roller of the genus
Eurystomus. Rollers are
relatively large tropical
birds.

latter species, popularly known as the dollar bird, has a spot on each wing resembling a coin. These rollers nest in hollow trees or in holes in the ground.

The Hoopoe, *Upupa epops,* is the only species of the family Upupidae. It is found in areas from Europe to South Africa, on the island of Madagascar, in India, Ceylon, Malaysia and on the Indonesian island of Sumatra.

Given such a dispersed distribution, this species has been divided into subspecies. These differ from one another by the intensity of their coloring which, if not spectacular, is quite elegant. The body is a pinkish-brown, with the brown varying in each subspecies.

The Wood Hoopoes of the family Phoeniculidae are often considered a subfamily of the Upupidae. However, since they live only in Africa and look so different from the true hoopoes, it is perhaps more accurate to classify these birds as a separate family. The wood hoopoes have no crest, their coloration is more uniform than that of other hoopoes. Their eggs are colored, unlike those of almost all other Coraciiformes.

There are six species grouped into three genera: *Phoeniculus, Scoptellus,* and *Rhinopomastus.* Their plumage is generally dark blue or green with metallic glints. The tail often has white patches around the tip, while the wings have a horizontal band that appears when they are spread in flight. The beaks come in a variety of colors: red, yellow, orange, and even black. The third and fourth toes are joined at the base.

Wood hoopoes are gregarious, and prefer to live in regions that are rich in bushes and trees. However, they avoid tropical rain forests. They prefer a diet of insects and rarely eat fruit or berries. Their nests are built in trees, and they usually lay three eggs at a setting.

The Hornbills of the family Bucerotidae include some of the most unusual birds. Eyelashes, which give them a somewhat human appearance, are a family trait. They have curious beaks, strange and varied calls, and an extremely noisy method of flight. The females have a survival strategy during the nesting period that is one of the strangest in the bird world: they wall themselves in.

The hornbills have huge, colorful, two-tiered beaks that are rather unwieldy looking and, in some species, are further adorned by a casquelike horny shell. Although this rather grotesque combination appears too heavy to permit flight, the casque is hollow, and the beak, which is honey-combed with air chambers, is almost as light as sponge rubber. This sensational ornament does not, however, seem to serve any practical purpose in the hornbill's life. The casque of the male black-casqued hornbill, *Ceratogymna atrata,* is so large that it almost engulfs the beak, which itself is enormous.

When in flight, certain hornbills employ a furious wing-flapping that produces a sound like a steam engine and can be heard a mile away. Each species has its own call: some bray like donkeys, some bark like dogs, others honk, toot, whistle, or squeal.

In addition to their unusual beaks and eyebrows, all hornbills share certain other characteristics. These unusual, large birds, which range in size from 16 to 60 inches, have typical coraciiform feet. The second, third, and fourth toes are joined, while the first or hind toe is free; each toe has a well-developed callus pad. As a rule, the birds' legs are short but sturdy. Their coloring is brown, black, or black and white. Another curious characteristic of the family is the

fusion of the vertebrae at the base of the neck of all the Bucerotidae.

The hornbill's fascinating nesting habits are unique in the bird world. The female lays three or five eggs as high as possible in the hollow of a tree. With the help of the male, the opening leading to the nest is sealed with excrement or clay, leaving only a narrow slit through which the male can pass food to the female. During this period of voluntary imprisonment, the female is lovingly tended by the male, who brings her food 10 to 20 times a day. The incuba-

Despite its clumsy appearance, the yellow-billed hornbill, an inhabitant of Africa, flies strongly. Unlike most of its family, this member of the genus Tockus *has no casque, or horn, on its beak.*

tion period is lengthy, as long as 40 days for the genus *Bycanistes*. The maturation period for the young is equally long; in some species the female remains enclosed for 110 days—nearly four months.

The nest is kept relatively clean, the female defecating neatly through the opening. When the young are ready to leave the nest, the female hammers down the wall with her beak and they emerge. The mother is so fat and flabby that she can scarcely fly. The female molts during this period of maternity confinement.

One variation in nesting habits is found in the genus *Tockus*. As soon as the female has shed her feathers, she opens a narrow passage in the wall and leaves the nest to help the male feed the nestlings. Mindful of dangerous predators, the young hornbills

close up the hole when the female has gone out. This variation is probably due to the carnivorous diet of the genus. Meat takes more time and effort to find than the fruits and insects eaten by other species, and the male needs the help of its mate to provide sufficient food, especially as the young get larger and require more nourishment.

The only apparent exception to these nesting habits occurs in the ground hornbills, which do not seal the female into the nest. Ground hornbills spend more time on the ground than most Bucerotidae. As a result of evolution they have higher ankles and shorter toes than their cousins.

The Bucerotidae are divided into two subfamilies: the Bucoracinae, with only two African species, and the Bucerotinae, which includes all other hornbills. Africa is the

This male red-billed hornbill (near right) feeds its mate during the incubation period of the eggs, which lasts 30 days. During this time, the female is literally sealed off from the rest of the world by a wall of excrement or clay, with only a small slit left open through which the male gives food to the female.

A great hornbill (far right) surveys the bottom of its cage. Its powerful bill can crunch a lizard or locust to pulp.

home of the majority of the hornbill family. Of the 25 species living there, some have very small casques, while others have very large ones. There are some 20 species from India to the Philippine Islands. Malaysia and India are the habitats of the great hornbill, *Buceros bicornis*, which reaches a length of almost 60 inches. It has a handsome yellow beak, a large casque, and black-and-white plumage.

The helmeted hornbill, *Rhinoplax vigil*, which inhabits the Far East, is the only species with a filled, or solid, casque. It is a little more than 3 inches long and once had considerable commercial value. The casque, which looks somewhat like a cross between amber and yellow jade, was called ivory. Records from ancient China indicate that it was worth more than jade or gold and had twice the value of a pound of elephant ivory.

The casques were imported into China, where artisans fashioned them into finely wrought belt buckles, snuff boxes, and plume holders. Some Borneo tribesmen still carve the casque, but their workmanship is relatively unsophisticated, and the art is dying out.

The Ethiopian ground hornbill, *Bucorvus abyssinicus*, roams the savannahs of East Africa. It lives on insects and has learned to hunt on the perimeter of brush fires started by natives as they clear the ground for cultivation. Insects fleeing from the fire are readily consumed by the waiting hornbills. The native population often embalms the heads of these birds, which they set atop their own heads as camouflage in order to speak through the brush of the savannah to approach herds of grazing animals.

The ground hornbill, *Bucorvus leadbeateri*, also ranges over the savannahs of Africa. About the size of a turkey, this bird has markedly long legs. Its inflatable throat sacs are another distinctive characteristic. The sac of the male is red, that of the female, blue. The diet of these hornbills is remarkably varied, ranging from other birds, snakes, small mammals, the remains of big animals, and frogs through seeds and fruits to such insects as beetles. The ground hornbill is well named; it is the most terrestrial member of the family. Its nesting sites are nearly as varied as its diet.

The white-crested hornbill, *Berenicornis albocristatus*, is found throughout western Africa. It follows troops of monkeys and lives on insects that these animals root out.

This young wreathed hornbill (right) has broken the tip of its upper bill. One of the species that lacks a casque on the bill, it has a furrowed, wrinkled mass at the base instead. This develops fully only in adults.

Woodpeckers and Others— Piciformes

The order Piciformes includes the woodpeckers, toucans, honeyguides, jacamars, barbets, and puff birds. All members of this order are equipped with zygodactylic feet—two toes pointing forward and two projecting backward. Individual families, however, are quite dissimilar.

Similarities among the families include hard, rather sparse, but brilliantly colored feathers; different coloring of the two sexes; and wings that are generally rounded. Nearly all members of this order live in trees, though some feed on the ground.

They resemble Coraciiformes in that they nest in the hollows of trees, and their eggs are always white. However, the reproductive habits of the honeyguides differ from those of the other Piciformes; they lay their eggs in the nests of other birds, particularly barbets and woodpeckers.

Piciformes live in the woods and forests of all the tropical and temperate regions of the world except Australia, New Zealand, and Madagascar. Where the order originated is not known. Fossils of members of the woodpecker family that date back 20 million years have been found in Europe and North America, but little is actually known of their evolution or of their relations with other bird families, except that they appear to be related to barbets.

The Jacamars of the family Galbulidae are among the more colorful inhabitants of the spectacular bird world of tropical America. There are about 15 species of jacamars in this region. They are notable for the metallic glints in their plumage, where green, gold, and copper shades predominate. These birds also prefer to feed on brightly colored insects, especially multicolored moths and dragonflies. Jacamars range in length from

5 to 12 inches, but most of this is accounted for by the beak and by the tail, which is usually pointed.

Jacamars are slender, noisy birds whose shrill note can be easily identified in the forest. Some species have a very melodious song. The colorful insects that are their preferred diet are generally caught in flight.

Nests are made in tunnels, sandbanks, and sometimes in heaps of earth among the exposed roots of trees that have been blown down in storms. Claybanks along rivers and termite mounds are also possible nesting sites. Two or four eggs are laid; these are incubated by both parents for three weeks. The male incubates them by day, the female by night. The young have a thick whitish down at birth.

Two of the largest hornbills are seen here. The rhinoceros hornbill (left) and the great hornbill (right). Both are Asian species that seal their mates into the nest during the incubation period. Both feed on fruits and small animals.

99

The largest species is the great jacamar, *Jacamerops aurea*. Its head is a brilliant green that shades into a golden bronze on the back; the color then grades to a golden green, which continues into the central feathers of the tail. The side feathers are a brilliant violet-blue; the throat is white, and the lower parts are light russet. This colorful species is found from Costa Rica in Central America to the Amazon Valley of South America.

Of the other species, the best known is probably the red-tailed jacamar, *Galbula ruficauda*. It is identical to the great jacamar except for a green stripe that separates the white of its throat from its russet-colored underparts. The red-tailed jacamar is found from southern Mexico to Brazil and on the island of Trinidad.

The Puffbirds of the family Bucconidae are a little-known group. Like a number of other tropical birds, they limit their territory to land areas in Central and South America; they never even cross the narrow strip of water to the islands of the Caribbean.

They appear to be closely related to jacamars. However, they are smaller. Their relatively large head and short beak give them an expanded look, although they never exceed 6 inches in length. They are quieter than jacamars; their coloring, while far more subdued, is nonetheless elegant. Until now only two kinds of nests have been observed. These are in holes dug in the soil and in termite nests in trees.

The nesting habits of puffbirds resemble those of the jacamars, except in the white-faced puffbird, where the male sits on the eggs during the night, and the young are hatched without down or feathers.

The Barbets belong to the family Capitonidae. Barbets are named after the tufts of feathers that trim the base of the beak and form a beard. This family of 13 genera contains 76 species, most of which live in Africa

and the Far East. A few species are also found in Central America and northern South America.

Barbets are not large, ranging in length from 4 to 13 inches. Their plumage consists of brightly colored greens, olives, browns, and blacks, with large patches of yellow, red, gray, or white decorating the head and breast.

This gay polka-dotted D'Arnaud's barbet (below) is found in Africa, where many members of the family make their home.

Barbets somewhat resemble the puffbirds in shape. But the beak is broader, stronger, and hooked. Their head is larger, their tail is shorter, and they are more active. Barbets are not migratory; they live and hunt in the dense woods of Asia and Africa, feeding on insects and fruits. They capture insects by perching on a branch until a passing insect appears, and then they hurtle after it.

A few species nest in small- to moderate-sized colonies, but individual couples generally care for their eggs. The two to four

Toucan barbets (opposite page), with their unusually heavy bill, are distinct among their clan. Representatives of the New World tropical genus Semnornis, *they frequent forested mountain slopes.*

white eggs are laid in a hole, which they excavate, in a hollow of a tree, or in a den built into a sandbank. Honeyguides often lay their eggs in the nests of barbets.

The Honeyguides of the family Indicatoridae have peculiar habits. They serve as guides for others in a common search for bees' nests. The honeyguide will escort another bird, an animal, or even a human to the source of honey. Once the bees' nest has been located and the honey removed, the honeyguide is free to feed on bits of remaining honeycomb. Beeswax is supposedly indigestible, but the bird has bacteria in its intestines that turn the wax into useful food.

The honeyguides are nest parasites, using the occupied nests of other birds for laying and hatching their eggs. The young are well-adapted to these parasitic habits; they are born with sharp hooks on their bill that are used to push out or kill the native residents of the nests. Once this task is accomplished, the hooks fall off. The parent honeyguide deposits only one egg in a nest. If more were laid, the nestlings would attempt to kill each other—despite their close relationship.

Most of the 11 species of honeyguides are found in Africa south of the Sahara Desert.

Two species, however, are found from the Himalayan mountains to Burma, Malaysia, and Borneo.

Their plumage is subdued and ranges from grays to brown and olive shades. Some species have yellow patches, and all species have a tail marked with white. One species has a harp-shaped tail. The beak is generally short and robust, and they have the zygodactyl feet common to all Piciformes. The structure of the plumage also places them in this order, in spite of the fact that in general appearance they are more similar to birds of the order Passeriformes.

Honeyguides live on the edges of forests where there is little vegetation but where they can hunt for the nests of bees and other insects.

The Toucans of the family Ramphastidae have a beak that is as unwieldly as that of the hornbill. Toucans are found in tropical forests and mountains from Central America to Argentina. Exactly why this huge lobster-claw beak evolved is not known. Perhaps it developed because the toucans feed on fruit. In any case, the beak is an excellent identifying feature and may be important in courtship displays. Despite its size, the beak

The spectacularly colored beak of the bird at right has a shape that explains its name, the keel-billed toucan.

The channel-billed toucan (far right) has a black bill and elegant black, yellow, and orange plumage.

is not heavy because it is honeycombed with air chambers.

Toucans range in size from 12 to 24 inches. Their plumage is brilliantly colored, and they are favorites in zoos.

Toucans vary in their flying ability. Some fly many miles in search of food. These birds, however, are very skillful climbers.

They nest in the hollows of trees or in holes dug by themselves or by other birds. They do not share the hornbill's strange habit of walling itself in. Rather, toucans are friendly birds, communicating with each other in hoarse, squawking cries. The feeding habits of the toucan are their least at-

tractive feature—they feed on the nestlings of other birds. Insects and lizards also are part of their diet.

The toucan family contains 5 genera with 37 species. The major genera are the true toucans of the genus *Ramphastos;* the aracaris, genus *Pteroglossus;* and the small toucanets, genus *Selenidera.*

The Woodpeckers belong to the family Picidae. Except in Australia, New Guinea, and Madagascar, these birds are found wherever there are trees. They can be found in parks, suburban gardens, and deserts, as well as in forests.

Woodpeckers are extraordinarily well-equipped for climbing trees and finding food beneath the bark. It is often difficult to see the woodpecker while it is pecking at a tree, but it can invariably be heard. During the mating season the sound is even more distinct, as the bird beats its familiar tatoo on the dead limbs of trees.

Woodpeckers have zygodactyl feet, with two toes in front and two in back. However, this does not seem to be an adaptation for climbing, since more specialized woodpeckers actually climb up the tree with 3 or even 4 toes pointing forward.

The tail plays a role in climbing; its feathers are stiff, almost rigid, and end in spines that enable the bird to brace itself against the tree and push upward. The woodpecker stops periodically, bracing itself with its tail, and starts digging for food beneath the bark. The woodpecker's beak, a highly developed tool, is chisel-tipped and strong. It is capable of gouging, drilling, and hammering for the kind of insects and larvae found in the trees of tropical and temperate forests.

The woodpecker also has a highly specialized tongue: it is long and can protrude a considerable distance out of the mouth, which assists the bird in its search for food. Generally, the tongue has a spiny tip resembling

The yellow-bellied sapsucker (above) drills rows of holes in the bark of trees. Then it sucks the sap that runs from the holes.

A male flicker (bottom), one of the commonest American woodpeckers, pauses at the entrance to its nest. The western races, such as that shown here, have red moustaches, whereas eastern North American males have black moustaches. Flickers feed on the ground, unlike most woodpeckers.

the tip of a harpoon or spear. The great spotted woodpecker has tiny barbs at the tip of its tongue. At its base, the tongue is attached to a hyoid system made up mainly of cartilage. This tough, white, fibrous connective tissue usually calcifies with maturation, but in the case of the woodpecker it remains cartilage and accounts for the lengthy protrusion of the tongue.

The hyoid system functions almost like a spring; it is coiled around the throat, the back part of the head, then up above the brain and, in a few species, into the right nostril. When the bird locates insect larvae

—an instinct that is not completely understood—it digs a hole with its scalpel-like beak and quickly inserts its tongue. The barb-tipped tongue is also coated with a sticky fluid that prevents the prey from escaping.

The plumage of the woodpeckers is colorful, with well-proportioned combinations of black, white, yellow, red, brown, and green; some have stripes and spots. Many species are decorated with crests and collars that are almost always a different color from the rest of the plumage.

Woodpeckers have somewhat uniform nesting habits. Most prefer specific kinds of trees for their nests.

The bird drills a hole in the tree, then lays its eggs on chips in the bottom of the cavity. These eggs are almost always a glowing white and number from two to eight, according to species.

The gila woodpecker of the southwestern United States digs holes in trees; in desert areas they use giant cacti, which when they dry out in the arid atmosphere become ideal nesting places. The rare ivory-billed woodpecker of the southeastern United States and Cuba nests in pines or cypress trees.

The family Picidae is divided into three subfamilies: the Picinae, which includes the real woodpeckers; the Picumninae, which includes the dwarf woodpeckers, or piculets; and the Jynginae, which includes the wrynecks. The wrynecks are quite prolific, and are capable of laying a total of 62 eggs in 62 days.

The genera of the subfamily Picinae with the most species include *Dendrocopos*, which is found on all continents except Australia and includes the European great spotted woodpecker; *Picus* of Eurasia; *Campethera* and *Dendropicos* of Africa; and *Melanerpes* of the New World. Other genera in the subfamily Picinae are *Chrysocolaptes*, which includes the golden-backed woodpecker of the Indo-Malaysian region; and *Campephilus*, the ivory-billed woodpeckers of the New World.

Poised at the hole of her nest, this female lesser spotted woodpecker of Europe is carrying food for her young. It is said that woodpeckers remove the wood chips made from the drilling of their tree holes and place them some distance from their nest to hide its location.

Campepfilus, found from Malaysia to Europe and America, includes all the largest woodpeckers.

The subfamily Picumninae includes approximately 28 species of piculets, very small birds whose tails lack the bracing supports found in birds of the preceding subfamily. Piculets are scattered throughout the Central and South American tropics, southern Asia, and Africa.

The subfamily Jynginae includes only two species. They are called wrynecks because they twist their necks slowly and very far around when surprised. Their plumage resembles tree bark and provides an excellent camouflage. The structure of their legs and tails makes them less well-adapted for climbing trees than the true woodpeckers. One species, *Jynx torquilla,* migrates from Europe south to Africa.

The wryneck (upper right) is a woodpecker relative that eats ants. It lives in Europe.

Despite its appearance, the woodpecker (lower left) is called the green woodpecker. This individual is a female.

A male black woodpecker (lower right) braces itself against a tree. This is the largest and rarest of the European woodpeckers.

Young green woodpeckers, downy and timid, are seen here in their nest. The red feathers that form such a large patch on the adult green woodpecker are just beginning to appear.

Songbirds or Perching Birds —Passeriformes

The last and the most extensive order of birds, the Passeriformes, or passerines, includes 5,500 of the 8,600 known species of living birds. The Passeriformes are the most specialized of the 27 orders of birds. It is also the only order that has shown successful adaptation to, and expanding distribution in, the latest phases of the earth's history.

The passerines, which include perching birds and songbirds, such as jays, blackbirds, finches, warblers, and sparrows, evolved only 60 million years ago. This is in sharp contrast to the waterfowl, whose ancestors date back 115 million years. It is probable that the process of specialization is still occurring at a rapid and steady pace, even to the extent of developing new species.

The Passeriformes are divided into four suborders. The first three—Eurylaimi, Tyranni and Menurae—are collectively described by some experts as sub-Oscines; the fourth suborder, which includes some 40 families, is the Oscines, or songbirds.

The main feature separating the Passeriformes in groups is the structure of the organs designed for singing. This method of grouping is the most logical since the Passeriformes, more than any other birds, have the greatest variety of calls and songs. And, for the most part, it is these calls and songs that are most familiar to man, for the passerines have adapted to human environments more successfully than any other birds. Their songs and calls are the result of membranes vibrating inside a vocal organ called the *syrinx*, which is found at the base of the *trachea*, or windpipe. These vibrations produce a voice, or bird call, whose pitch can be changed by activating various muscles.

The feet are an important feature of similarity among the Passeriformes. Each foot has the usual four toes, each of which is connected at points on a single plane. The backward position of the hind toe enables members of this order to perch securely and gracefully on materials of any density—from thick branches to telephone wires to delicate leaf stems. As in many other birds the tendons that control the bending of these four toes are arranged so that the toes can lock around a perch. Any movement that threatens the equilibrium of a perching bird automatically assures that the toes will grip more surely. As a result, such fragile birds as the robin and chaffinch can sleep as they perch—not even a strong wind will dislodge them. In the Passeriformes the toes are never joined by a membrane, even in species with aquatic habits.

Molting is accomplished in a methodical, symmetrical fashion. The essential flight feathers always shed equally on both sides, to prevent reduction in flying capacity. All species have either nine or ten flight feathers.

The differences that do exist among the passerines are the result of the adaptations of various genera to the demands of their habitat. The beak, for instance, has become adapted to the kinds of food favored by each bird. The soft, slender body shape of the average passerine is suited to both a flesh and vegetable diet. However, the beaks vary widely. A conical and often massive beak is required for taking semihard foods; a smaller, wide-throated beak, like that of the swallow, is adapted to seizing insects in flight. Some Passeriformes feed principally on nectar and pollen and, therefore, have a slender, curved beak with a special tongue structure. Other species are predators and possess strong, hooked beaks.

There is great variation of size among the Passeriformes; some wrens measure only 3 inches in length, while the lyrebird, with its tail, can exceed 40 inches. The coloring and ornamentation of the plumage are equally varied, some having remarkable richness of hue and pattern.

The brambling Fringilla montifringilla (opposite page) is a species of finch. It lives in northern Europe.

The Passeriformes are essentially land birds. A few species find their food exclusively in the water, but they never venture very far upon it. For them, the open sea represents the worst of perils during their migrations. Migratory behavior is especially highly developed in many species of this order, particularly those insectivorous, or insect-eating, birds that nest at high latitudes. The tropical species generally remain in their habitat the year around, except sometimes in areas with pronounced wet and dry seasons during the year.

The Passeriformes in general enjoy a great variety of environments, including deserts and mountain ranges with little vegetation.

Some species have successfully adapted themselves to environments created by man; for instance, they can live in tilled fields, or nest or sleep in urban areas, where they have learned to eat many foods other than those provided directly by nature.

The coloration of their eggs is also amazingly varied. But in all cases the young must live in the nest and are born totally helpless. Parental care is the general rule, except in a few species of the families Estrildidae, Ploceidae, and Icteridae, which prefer to let foster parents hatch and rear their young.

The division of the Oscines into families is somewhat arbitrary, because the re-

The soft browns and grays of this hedge sparrow, or dunnock, as well as its physical shape, are typical of a member of the order Passeriformes.

semblances among the various species are so great, and the effects of adaptive or convergent characteristics are so marked. It is extremely difficult to find real lines of kinship among the various groups. The lines of demarcation are shadowy and are further blurred by the presence of aberrant forms whose inclusion in, or exclusion from, a given family is a matter of each naturalist's personal opinion.

Thus, the thrushes, warblers, and flycatchers of the Old World have long been regarded as sufficiently different to warrant their placement in separate families: the Turdidae; Sylviidae, and Muscicapidae, respectively. But when their species are examined from a worldwide point of view, such differences are less important, and these birds are now sometimes classified as subfamilies of the Muscicapidae.

Other valid doubts concern the criteria for distinguishing between the Fringillidae and the Emberizidae, which are often placed in a single family. A few of the families, such as the larks and the swallows, are well characterized. One point on which the two schools of American and European classification are divided is the position of the Corvidae. European authorities place it at the end of the entire class because, while it may be true that its members are not the most recently evolved of the Passeriformes, as the Americans contend, the fact remains that they show maximum development of mental faculties. Others feel that more specialized, recently evolved families belong near the end of the order.

The Passeriformes are a cosmopolitan order and are found everywhere except in truly polar regions and the most remote islands. Some groups have a worldwide distribution, while others are extremely limited. The suborder Oscines, for example, is represented everywhere. Many of its families are cosmopolitan, or at least widely distributed in the Eastern or Western Hemisphere.

Passeriformes
Suborder
Eurylaimi
   Eurylaimidae
Suborder
Tyranni
   Dendrocolaptidae
   Furnariidae
   Formicariidae
   Conopophagidae
   Rhinocryptidae
   Pittidae
   Philepittidae
   Xenicidae
   Tyrannidae
   Pipridae
   Cotingidae
   Phytotomidae

Suborder
Menurae
   Menuridae
   Atrichornithidae
Suborder
Oscines

Alaudidae	*Zosteropidae*
Hirundinidae	*Meliphagidae*
Motacillidae	*Emberizidae*
Campephagidae	*Thraupidae*
Pycnonotidae	*Parulidae*
Irenidae	*Drepanididae*
Laniidae	*Vireonidae*
Vangidae	*Icteridae*
Bombycillidae	*Fringillidae*
Dulidae	*Estrildidae*
Cinclidae	*Ploceidae*
Troglodytidae	*Sturnidae*
Mimidae	*Oriolidae*
Prunellidae	*Dicruridae*
Muscicapidae	*Callaeidae*
Paridae	*Grallinidae*
Sittidae	*Artamidae*
Certhiidae	*Cracticidae*
Climacteridae	*Ptilinorhynchidae*
Dicaeidae	*Paradisaeidae*
Nectariniidae	*Corvidae*
Hypocoliidae	*Ptilogonatidae*

Warblers have slender bills, well adapted to their insectivorous diet.

Sparrows have short, conical bills which are ideal for their mixed diet of insects and grains.

Hawfinches have short, powerful bills, conical in shape, which are needed in cracking the hard seeds which make up their diet.

Crossbills have pointed, crossed mandibles which serve as a perfect specialized tool for opening pine cones and extracting the seeds.

Other families, however, are much more confined in their distribution, sometimes restricted to areas such as Madagascar, New Zealand, or Hawaii. The Pittidae of the suborder Tyranni are quite widely distributed in the tropical zones of the Eastern Hemisphere; the Philepittidae are limited to Madagascar; and the Xenicidae are peculiar to New Zealand. The suborder Eurylaimi, on the other hand, is Afro-Asian, and the families that constitute the suborder Menurae are exclusively Australian.

The Broadbills of the family Eurylaimidae are the only members of the suborder Eurylaimi. They include 14 species that range in length from 5 to 11 inches. The head is rather large, with a broad, flat bill that in some species is partly hidden by a short crest. The eyes, which are relatively large, give evidence of forest-dwelling habits.

The major species belong to the genera *Calyptomena*, *Eurylaimus*, and *Psarisomus*. These are all found throughout the Orient, from India to Malaysia. The species of the

Weavers or weaverbirds (below) weave nests out of grasses. They build them on the tips of slender branches. When completed, the nests have an entrance tube leading to the actual living quarters.

genus *Smithornis* belong exclusively to Africa and are distinguished not only by their small size but also by their appearance, whose subdued color is similar to a flycatcher's.

In the Asian species, on the other hand, very bright colors predominate—a great deal of green and blue or glossy black, wine red, and various zones of contrasting colors, including yellow, orange, gray, or chestnut. In addition, many species have a white patch on the back that is especially noticeable in flight.

As a rule, broadbills are quiet creatures that prefer the shaded areas of tropical forests. Here they hunt insects, frogs, and small lizards, and eat an occasional fruit.

The broadbill generally hangs its nests over rivers. A pear-shaped structure, interwoven with grasses and decorated with moss, it resembles a piece of driftwood. The nest-building indicates an astute instinct for judging the level of the river waters in time of flood. The water level may be far below the nest when the broadbill starts to build, but when the waters rise, the nest is still safely positioned.

The Suborder Tyranni contains 12 families that differ from the other Passeriformes by a certain "primitiveness." The pattern of the plumage is usually rather coarse and, in comparison to the other Passeriformes, the coloration is somewhat more subdued and less varied. The structure of the musculature of the syrinx is less complex and does not allow an elaborate song, even though it may be sonorous.

The Woodcreepers of the family Dendrocolaptidae include 48 species found from Mexico to Argentina. These birds vary in length from 6 to 14 inches, all with rather modest plumage that is predominantly olive-brown, gray, or cinnamon. The plumage is streaked, or occasionally banded, and often bears a series of spots, especially on the

shoulders, wings, tail, and lower areas. The tail has a rigid pointed stabilizer, and the strong beak is quite long. These birds generally climb trees using the tail as a brace, like the woodpeckers. Their diet, in addition to insects and spiders, consists of small arboreal amphibians.

Woodcreepers nest in hollows, whether natural or made by other birds, and in other well-protected spots. They lay two or three white eggs, which both parents incubate. Though partly covered with down at birth, the young are completely helpless.

The Ovenbirds belong to the family Furnariidae. The nests of some species inspired the common name for the whole family. Members of the genus *Furnarius* build a hollow ball made of cow dung and mud, which resembles a primitive oven. Other members of the family build different types of nests. For example, some species, which are called twig gatherers, build enormous nests, often in cacti.

Aside from their nests and certain other external observations, not much is known about this family of Passeriformes, despite the large number of species—about 220. They can be found in wooded and open areas of South America, where they have adapted to a wide range of habitats from sea level to alpine plateaus.

Varying in length from 5 to 9 inches, the Furnariidae have dark-brown, olive-brown, or cinnamon-brown plumage. Each bird is generally uniform in color, though some species do have stripes, spots, or scale patterns. In most instances, the beak is rather narrow and the shape of the tail is variable. The legs are always strong, but of medium length. There is considerable diversity, however, in physiological activities. The vocalizations in particular are widely varied, from short, sharp sounds to resonant, modulated ones. One species, Hudson's spinetail, *Asthenes hudsoni*, has a mourning song, while the cachalotes of the genus *Pseudoseisura* emit especially cacaphonous, piercing sounds.

While most species of Furnariidae are insectivorous, some are seed-eaters, and those of the genus *Cinclodes* also eat small crustaceans and other water animals.

Characteristic of the family are white-colored eggs, with the single exception of the marsh-dwelling species *Phleocryptes melanops*, whose eggs are bright blue. While reproductive habits vary widely within the family, the eggs usually number from three to five, and are deposited in holes in the ground, either natural or built by the birds. Some have covered nests.

The sharp-tailed streamcreeper, *Lochmias nematura*, forages among the flotsam that gathers along the banks of streams emptying into large rivers. Species of the genus *Cinclodes* are always found in open country in the vicinity of water, hunting for food along the shore. There are also swamp species, such as the curved-bill reed haunter, *Limnornis curvirostris*.

The North American ovenbird is really a wood warbler, belonging to the family Parulidae and the genus *Seiurus*.

The reddish-colored ovenbird (right) is a member of a chiefly South American family that has adapted to many regions. Some ovenbirds live in hot, tropical jungles; others on the vast, dry, grassy pampas of Argentina; still others on the rocky mountain slopes of Chile.

The Antbirds of the family Formicariidae include 230 species found exclusively in Central and South America. The family's name comes from those species that accompany hordes of swarming army ants to feed on the insects that are routed by the ants during their marches. None of the species feed on ants, though most are insectivorous.

Varied in size, these birds range from 4 to 15 inches in length. Their rather loosely attached feathers run to black, gray, or

brown tones; the plumage is streaked or striped in white.

The antbird's nest is usually an open cup hanging from branches, but some species nest in the shelter of thick grasses. Antbirds lay two or three eggs, which are a whitish color speckled with brown, red, or black patches.

The Antpipits of the family Conopohagidae are another exclusively South American family. They are found from Colombia to Brazil. The plumage of these tiny birds runs to brown and olive green, the breast and stomach feathers to white and light brown. The head and throat are brightly colored, and the eyes are outlined in white. They belong to the Passeriformes by virtue of the characteristic formation of the syrinx.

The Tapaculos are members of the family Rhinocryptidae. The common name of this neotropical family is from the Spanish, and is derived from the bird's habit of elevating its tail when excited. Tapaculos live in the undergrowth of dense forests where they prefer to run about—rather than fly—in search of food; their diet consists almost exclusively of insects. Some species build a domed nest in high grass, but most nest in the hollows of sandbanks, rocks, or trees.

The Pittas belong to the family Pittidae. They are one of the few families in the suborder Tyranni not found in the Western Hemisphere. The pittas are numerous in Africa and in the Far East from India to the Solomon Islands. They are most heavily concentrated in Indo-Malayan regions.

Pittas eat both plant and animal material, which they find on the forest floor. Although infrequently seen, their distinctive calls—an assortment of whistles, squawks, and grunts—are well-known to ornithologists.

Varying in length from 6 to 11 inches, the pitta's plumage is generally contrasting and brightly colored in combinations of red, blue, green, and violet. Most species resemble short-tailed thrushes to such an extent that the brilliant plumage and thrush-like qualities of one have given it the name jewel-thrush.

The Asities of the family Philepittidae are found in Madagascar. They are similar to the pittas in the structure of the syrinx, and are considered by many authorities to be Madagascar's equivalent to the Pittidae.

The family includes two genera, each with

two species. The velvet asity and Schlegel's asity comprise the genus *Philepitta*, while the two species of false sunbirds are placed in the genus *Neodrepanis*.

The New Zealand Wrens are members of the family Xenicidae. These small, 3- to 4-inch wrens live in the trees and shrubs of the now-diminishing New Zealand forest. Members of the four known species are poorly equipped for flying because of their short, rounded wings. One species, now extinct, was apparently completely flightless.

The blue-winged or fairy pitta is found from the southern regions of Japan to south China, the northern rim of India and Malaysia. It spends its days on the forest floor, searching out the grubs and insects on which it feeds.

The American, or Tyrant, Flycatchers of the family Tyrannidae include more than 350 species found throughout the Americas. Many of these birds catch their food by taking off from the branch of a tree in a swift but uneven flight and returning as soon as possible with their food. Flycatchers are primarily insectivorous.

They range in length from 3 to 9 inches. The plumage is almost always gray, brown, or olive green; in some species, it is striped. There is often a bright yellow, red, or white patch on the top of the head. The flat, slightly hooked beak is flanked on either side by rigid whiskers. Flycatchers' nests may be cup-shaped, spherical, or conical; they can be found in the branches and hollows of trees, in holes in the ground, or among tall reeds. While flycatchers have a wide variety of calls and notes, they do not produce a true song. They are pugnacious birds, hence the name tyrant flycatchers.

Common North American species are the kingbird; the phoebe, which often attaches

The umbrella-bird (above) is a cotinga. It has an umbrellalike crest and a breast wattle as long as its body.

The brilliant cock-of-the-rock (opposite page and near left) and the Peruvian cock-of-the-rock (far left) also are cotingas. They are among the most spectacular of birds. Unlike other cotingas, they construct shelflike nests on the wall of a cave or overhanging ledge.

its mud nest to a beam in an old shed; and the brilliant vermilion flycatcher.

Manakins of the family Pipridae are known for their complicated courtship rituals. The males flaunt themselves in a series of acrobatic movements in special arenas within which each claims its own territory. The females are always present to observe the scene, and occasionally contribute their own movements to the ritual.

These tiny birds are quite chunky, with short wings and tails; the beak is broad and hooked at the tip. The males are black with vivid red, orange, and blue flecks, while the females are greenish and less brilliantly plumed. The female builds the nest.

Members of this family, which includes 59 species, live in the moist, tropical forests of Central and South America.

The Cotingas are members of the family Cotingidae. It is one of the most diversified of all bird families in the Western Hemisphere. Some species have a bizarre growth of feathers on their wings and around the head. There are also wattles which in some species may be as long as the body. In other species the wattles assume equally odd forms; the bearded bellbird, for example, has three wattles. Many species are dull or undistinguished, but the male cock-of-the-rock is a spectacular orange or red bird whose flattened crest completely hides the beak and sail-shaped feathers.

Cotingas inhabit a wide region, beginning with the southern borders of Arizona (the only species appearing in the United States is the rose-throated becard, *Platypsaris aglaiae*) and extending down through two-thirds of South America. However, since they rarely descend from the tree tops to make themselves visible, little can be concluded concerning their habits except for the distinctive calls that resound through their densely wooded habitat.

The hooded pitta (above) and the blue-winged pitta (opposite page) are members of the family Pittidae. They have the strong feet of ground-foraging birds.

Cotingas are solitary birds. However, recent studies reveal that male cocks-of-the-rock gather in special arenas in forest clearings where they court their mates. The extraordinary wattles and distinctive calls of other species are thought to be prime sources of mate attraction. Once mates have been selected, the nest is built in tree branches or cemented to rocky surfaces with mud.

The eggs vary according to species. A female lays from one to six eggs, which range in color from white to dark brown, with various degrees of spotting. Males of some species take absolutely no part in the process of nesting.

While there is obviously considerable variety among species, there are some features that are fairly uniform: large, hooked beaks, rounded wings, and short, sturdy legs. All feed chiefly on fruit and insects.

The Plantcutters of the family Phytotomidae include three species, which are found only in South America. Their short, conical beaks have finely serrated edges that are admirably suited to cutting away fruits, buds, and leaves from trees. Their short, heavy bodies and long tails are similar to those of a finch, but they are closely related to the Tyrannidae.

The Suborder Menurae includes birds whose vocal muscles are similar to those of the Oscines, while the horny covering on the lower part of the leg resembles that of the Tyranni. There are only two families in this suborder; they are both found only in Australia.

The Lyrebirds of the family Menuridae are well-known for their tail, which is shaped like a lyre. These birds have solitary habits and are ground-living, since they prefer running to flying. The male constructs heaps of vegetable matter, on which it performs elaborate dances that draw attention to its magnificent

tail. These dances are accompanied by spirited singing.

The Scrub-birds of the family Atrichornithidae are the other members of the suborder Menurae. Their tail is very normal, and at first glance, they don't seem to belong in the same group as the lyrebird. Bird authorities, however, have discovered so many anatomical similarities that the scrub-birds are now considered to be the older members of the suborder with the lyrebird evolving later.

The Suborder Oscines includes about 40 families. Their classification is often disputed by ornithologists; but for the sake of clarity, one of the most common systems is used here. The Oscines include those songbirds with the most highly developed vocal organs.

The Larks of the family Alaudidae include about 75 species; only one reaches the New World. The rest of the species are distributed throughout Europe, central Asia, and Africa. The horned, or shore, lark, *Eremophila alpestris*, is found in North and South America. It has been able to adapt so well to so many different environments that many geographic races have evolved.

In most larks the feathers are gray-brown or ochre, with dark streaks on the top part of the body, and paler, less-spotted streaks beneath. One species, the black calandra lark, *Melanocorypha calandra*, is totally black. Some species have crests and tufts, but their coloring matches their environment, providing them with camouflage.

Larks are sociable birds and live in large groups. The horned lark prefers open farm land and prairie country, where it can be seen running along roads or soaring skyward. Most species of larks have a delightful song, which is best delivered from the air. The skylark, *Alauda arvensis*, is one of the most celebrated songsters in the world.

Unfortunately, the horned lark likes wheat seeds, which it consumes in great quantities. This incurs the anger of farmers, and larks are occasionally hunted and killed—a wasteful practice, since these birds also consume harmful insects and the seeds of weeds.

Larks build scanty, makeshift nests, always on the ground. The clutch size varies from three to five, depending on the climate of the species' habitat.

The Swallows of the family Hirundinidae are a widespread and familiar family of 75 species. Members of this group include the familiar barn swallow and the house, sand and crag martins. These birds range in length from 4 to 9 inches, and have brown, black, dark-green, or blue feathers that are often decorated with metallic highlights. Some are heavily striped, while others have white or russet backs. The lower parts are generally white or gray-brown, frequently marked with a dark pectoral band and reddish throat.

The head is generally quite big and flat, with a short, broad beak whose very wide opening is a most efficient insect trap. The swallow has a short neck and a long body. The wings are long and pointed, and produce a strong and rapid flight. The tail may be short, long, square, or even deeply forked, depending on the demands of local conditions. Sometimes the ankles of the very short legs are feathered.

Swallows feed only on insects, and indeed the presence of these birds is linked to the abundance of insects in the air. As the insects disappear with the approach of cold weather, thousands of swallows assemble to prepare for their trip south in search of food. With the approach of spring, swallows instinctively return just as insects emerge, thus explaining why swallows enjoy the well-deserved reputation as harbingers of spring. Consequently, they also symbolically represent the promise of happiness.

Almost all swallows are gregarious and typically aerial in their habits. The small insects that constitute their diet are almost always captured in the air. But swallows can easily perch on branches, wires, or the ground.

Many species use mud and other materials to build nests of various shapes. Some, however, lay their eggs in natural hollows of rocks or trees, while others dig holes in sandbanks, particularly on the banks of rivers. The number of eggs ranges from three to seven, according to species. In some cases, they are incubated by both sexes; in others, only by the female. In view of their manner of feeding, the young do not leave the nest until they are completely capable of flight.

During the mating season, the tail of the lyrebird (right) is spread and brought forward over the back. As part of its courting ritual, the lyrebird mimics the calls of other birds.

Swallows are found throughout the world except at very high altitudes and on some oceanic islands.

The Wagtails and Pipits of the family Motacillidae constitute a group of about 50 species whose distribution is cosmopolitan. These are small birds, ranging from 5 to 9 inches in length. They have long wings and tails. The beak, of varying length, is always rather slender. The hind toe is longer than that of most birds.

All Motacillidae have predominantly terrestrial habits, even though they often perch in trees. Many species engage in regular migrations. Their plumage may be uniformly black, gray, brown, olive green, or yellow; the yellow is found particularly in the wagtails of the genera *Motacilla* and *Budytes*. In the pipits, particularly of *Anthus* and related genera, coloring is variously streaked and spotted. In this family the lower parts may be uniform in color or marked by streaks of white, black, ochre, or yellow.

Almost all Motacillidae are gregarious, except during the reproductive period. In many species the birds habitually move the tail up and down, whether at rest or in motion. Their flight is often characteristically undulant. In the genus *Anthus* in particular,

Two adult horned larks (above) are feeding their young. This is the only member of the lark family that has reached North America.

The colors and shape of this skylark (left) are ideal for camouflage in its natural environment.

A member of the familiar swallow family, the bird seen above is the sand martin, or bank swallow. These birds, found throughout the world, are migratory.

there is an elaborate courtship flight during which the males sing melodiously. Their diet consists of insects, spiders, and mollusks. The cup-shaped nest is built on the ground or in the hollows of rocks, walls, or trees.

The species that shows the greatest diversity of plumage according to its geographical distribution is the yellow wagtail, *Motacilla flava*. When these birds assume their courting plumage, the males have different markings on the head, ranging from yellow to ash-gray. The variety of popular and local names, such as blue-headed wagtail, suggests misleadingly that many different species or subspecies of *M. flava* exist; this is probably not true.

The Cuckoo-shrikes of the family Campephagidae vary in length from 5 to more than 12 inches. They are characterized by a soft plumage that is not firmly attached to the skin. Their coloration varies from gray-brown to black, including blue, red, orange, or yellow in various combinations. There is prominent striping on the lower parts of some species; other species are white or chestnut below. Sometimes the throat and breast are gray or black. The tail, generally uniform throughout the species, is tipped with white, yellow, orange or red. In many species, the back is striped, or it is lighter than the rest of the upper parts. The moderately long beak is quite strong and often markedly hooked. Two species belonging to the genus *Campephaga* have orange wattles at the junction of the jaws. The legs are usually short.

The geographical distribution of the family is very wide, extending from Africa across India to Japan, the Philippines, and Australia. In most instances, the species are sedentary, typical inhabitants of not overly thick tropical forests, with essentially arboreal and often gregarious habits. The nest, which many species line with lichens and scraps of bark, is a shallow cup, generally built on horizontal branches at a certain height above the ground. The 70 species are divided into nine genera.

The minivets of the genus *Pericrocotus* are among the most richly colored species of the Campephagidae. In groups of about 20, these birds scour the tops of tall trees in search of food. They are often accompanied by birds of other families, such as flycatchers, warblers, and babblers. It is difficult to observe them because of the thick lower growths. Only when the flocks move about within the confines of a solitary valley is it possible to get a clear, unimpeded view of their blue-black and bright-orange coloring. Their courtship choreography is remarkable, as are the various calls that the male utters. It was formerly believed that each male had a small harem, so that locally these birds became known as sultan birds.

The Bulbuls of the family Pycnonotidae are Asian and African birds. They are generally found in tropical regions, usually in dense forests but sometimes in sparse or desert areas. This large family has about 15 genera and 120 species. They are smallish birds, ranging in size from that of a sparrow to a robin. Bulbuls are generally drab in appearance, with some dull green and bright yellow or scarlet about the tail. Many species have more or less inconspicuous crests. They eat mostly fruit and berries; several species, however, are insect-eaters. Their behavior ranges from the shy and secretive species of the dense forests to the bold dooryard species, some being common even in city parks. Many have loud, musical songs. A typical genus is represented by *Pycnonotus barbatus*, the black-eyed bulbul, which, with its many subspecies, is very common in Africa.

The Leafbirds of the family Irenidae are found in southern China, the Philippines, and Malaysia. This family has only three genera, each quite different from the others, although all are characterized by stout legs,

The European house martin (top) and the sand martin (center) are both swallows. As its name implies, the house martin nests on buildings.

small feet, and slender, slightly hooked bills.

Members of the genus *Aegithina*, the ioras, are the smallest of the leafbirds—about the size of chickadees. They are generally yellowish-green and black. Probably the best known species is *A. tiphia*, the common iora, frequently seen about houses. The golden-fronted leafbird, *A. aurifrons*, is often kept as a caged bird.

The second genus, *Chloropsis*, contains larger birds, dressed in a brighter green, frequently with splashes of orange, blue, or black. The third genus, *Irena*, contains the beautiful fairy-bluebirds, which have striking blue and black plumages. Most leafbirds live in forests where they eat fruit and insects. They are chattering birds, with many striking calls.

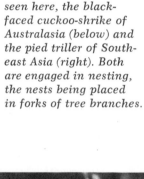

Two cuckoo-shrikes are seen here, the black-faced cuckoo-shrike of Australasia (below) and the pied triller of Southeast Asia (right). Both are engaged in nesting, the nests being placed in forks of tree branches.

The Shrikes are members of the family Laniidae. Two very similar species of this family—the widespread northern shrike, *Lanius excubitor*, and the loggerhead shrike, *L. ludovicianus*—are found in North America; all other members of this family are confined to Europe and Asia.

The family Laniidae contains four subfamilies: the Laniinae, or true shrikes; the Prionopinae, or helmet shrikes; the Malaconotinae, or bush shrikes; and the Pityriasinae, whose sole species is the bristlehead, *Pityriasis gymnocephala*, found only in Borneo. Many authorities do not consider any subfamily but the Laniinae, or true shrikes, as properly belonging to this family; but all show the chief characteristics of the shrikes.

They are aggressive, predatory birds, with sturdy hooked beaks and strong claws used for holding their prey. Many shrikes hang their prey on thorns, barbed wire, or tree branches, in part to help in the killing but also to provide a cache to which they can return again and again. The true shrikes normally perch on a tree or bush overlooking

open country; in flying, they drop suddenly to within a few feet of the ground before rising sharply to another perch.

The northern shrike is about the size of a robin. It is generally pale gray with a black mask across the face and black wings and tail. The loggerhead shrike is a little smaller, darker in color, with the black face mask reaching the bill.

The Vangas of the family Vangidae are sometimes called vanga-shrikes. They are found only in Madagascar. There are 12 species, which are characterized by heavy bills with hooks on the ends. They feed exclusively on insects and small animals that inhabit trees, such as tree frogs and lizards. Authorities speculate that the vangas are closely related to true shrikes, but became isolated in Madagascar and diverged into "new" species.

The bill of the vanga is heavier than that of the shrike, and in some species has become much enlarged and compressed laterally. In others the bill is thin and curved. Vangas are usually black or blue or white, with reddish-browns and grays mixed in. Most species flock readily and move together through the trees in search of food.

The Waxwings of the family Bombycillidae consist of three species that are widely distributed across the Northern Hemisphere from North America to East Asia. Their family name refers to their silky plumage. *Bombyx* in Latin means "silkworm." The common name derives from the red, waxlike tips on the secondary flight feathers.

Waxwings are brownish with darker wings slashed with white or white and yellow, and tipped with yellow or red. They have black masks, distinctive crests, and slightly hooked bills. In length they range from 6 to 8 inches.

The Bohemian waxwing, *Bombycilla garrulus,* is found in the evergreen forests of northwest North America, northern Europe, and in certain forest regions of Asia. Its wing

markings are bolder yellows, blacks, and reds. Sociable in their habits, these birds wander in nomadic flocks to more southerly regions at intervals of from four to seven years, presumably when their food—fruits and berries—becomes scarce.

The cedar waxwing, *B. cedrorum* is more widespread in North America. It is about 6 inches long, has a yellowish belly, and less conspicuous wing markings. Its call is a high monotone.

The Japanese waxwing, *B. japonica,* is native to eastern Siberia. Its red-tipped (rather than yellow-tipped) tail feathers and the crimson bar across the upper wing coverts distinguish it from the other species.

Usually the waxwing builds its loosely constructed nest in low trees. This nest, consisting of twigs lined with moss, grasses, and feathers, holds three to seven eggs, which are grayish blue with small black dots.

The yellow wagtail (above) eats an insect. The bird's name is derived from its habit of constantly "wagging" its tail.

The Palmchat, *Dulus dominicus,* is the only member of the family Dulidae. It is found in Haiti and the Dominican Republic. A sociable tree-dweller, it builds a rather large nest with a number of compartments circling the trunk of the royal palm. In the nest are various incubation chambers; in each chamber a different female lays four white eggs with coarse spots. Several couples collaborate in building this nest. Berries and flowers are the staple diet of the palmchat.

The Silky Flycatchers of the family Ptilogonatidae are found in North and Central America. They are closely related to the waxwings and palmchats. The slender birds of this family resemble flycatchers. They feed mainly on insects.

The Hypocolius, *Hypocolius ampelinus,* is the only member of the family Hypocoliidae. It is found in the Middle East. Like the silky flycatchers, *Hypocolius* is also closely related to the waxwings and palmchats.

The Dippers of the family Cinclidae are found near rapid mountain streams in Europe, Asia, and North and South America. They can forage for food on the surface as well as on the bottoms of these streams; their thick, oily plumage protects them from the cold waters. When foraging, the dippers fly quickly into rapidly flowing waters to swim or to walk on the bottom in search of larvae and snails.

There are four species in the genus *Cinclus,* and they are all similar in appearance. They are 5 to 8 inches long, their plumage is gray, brown, or black, and they are sometimes spotted with white patches. The compact body has a short tail and short wings, but the legs are long and sturdy, befitting a bird that must resist the strong currents of mountain streams. There are two New World species. One, the water ouzel, *C. mexicanus,* ranges from the far north to Panama.

The nest is a globular structure of grass, moss, and lichen, all finely interwoven. The nest, which has a side entrance, is frequently placed directly below a waterfall or even among the rocks or stumps in the very center of a river. The eggs, from three to seven, are a clear white and are incubated by the female only. Both parents, however, feed the young.

The Wrens belong to the family Troglodytidae. While they are familiar birds in North America, a greater number are found in Central and South America. Their familiarity results from the inclination of the house wren, *Troglodytes aedon,* and Bewick's wren, *Thryomanes bewickii,* to nest in bird houses. The house wren, the most common and most widely distributed American species, is found from Quebec to Argentina. Bewick's wren has been ejected from many areas by the smaller house wren, but it remains common in certain localities.

The 63 species of the family Troglodytidae have unmistakable, compact bodies, 4 to 9 inches long. Their multicolored plumage is characterized by red, gray, and brown coloration, varyingly striped, spotted, and interlaced with black and white, particularly on the wings, flanks, and tail. The tail is very long in some species and very short in others. It is almost always carried in an erect position.

All species in this family are confined to the Western Hemisphere, with the single exception of the common winter wren, *Troglodytes troglodytes,* which is widely distributed through Europe, the U.S.S.R., China, and Japan, as well as large areas of the United States and Canada. In all, nine species of wrens are found in North America.

As a rule, wrens prefer to live near water, but there are species in semidesert scrub areas. The largest wrens belong to a group of species known as the Cactus wrens. One of these birds builds its domed nests in cactus holes and other desert vegetation.

Generally well-constructed, the troglodytid nest may be placed among rocks, in the hollow of a tree or building, or even in grass, among reeds, or in a bush. In many species, the males build a number of unlined roosting nests, which are not used for breeding. The male marsh wren begins work on several nests as part of his courtship practices. One of these is ultimately selected by the female for use. The eggs are various colors; from two to ten eggs are laid, according to the species.

Songs of the wrens are elaborate and quite beautiful. While their short wings do not permit strong flight in most species, wrens are lively birds and very agile.

The Mockingbirds, Catbirds, and Thrashers of the family Mimidae are often referred to as "mimic thrushes" because of their ability to imitate other birds. The mockingbird not only mimics other birds but other animals as well. A mockingbird living in California can imitate a California tree frog or woodpecker, while a Kentucky mockingbird can mimic the frog sounds and woodpeckers of its region. There are 34 species in this family of typically American birds, found from Canada to southern Argentina.

The Mimidae resemble thrushes, with a much more prominent tail, which is often as long as the body. The plumage is gray-blue, gray, brown, or reddish above, while the lower parts are lighter, often white. A num-

One of the largest and most variable group of Old World songbirds is the so-called babblers. The black-capped sibia, shown here, is a babbler found in the higher wooded slopes of the Himalayan Mountains.

ber of species have brown or black patches, spots, or streaks, particularly below, and one species is completely glossy black.

The rather strong beak is generally quite long and is curved either slightly or markedly. The iris is often pale yellow, orange, or red. The wings are usually short and rounded, and the legs rather long.

The Mimidae build large, cup-shaped nests in bushes or on the ground. The female usually lays two to five pastel-colored eggs, which are hatched singly in most species; in certain of the thrashers, the male helps with the hatching. Both males and females vigorously defend the nest site against all intruders.

The rather varied diet consists of insects, fruits, berries, and seeds. Most species are bush- or tree-dwellers, but many feed on the ground.

The American catbird, *Dumetella caro-linensis,* a widespread species, has a distinctive call that sounds like a mewing cat.

The Hedge Sparrows, or Accentors, of the family Prunellidae are found exclusively in the Old World. This is a small family of only 12 species, all members of genus *Prunella.* Ranging in size from 5 to 7 inches, their plumage is brown, gray, and chestnut in various combinations. The upper parts are generally striped, and the lower are spotted or solid-colored. Frequently sociable and predominantly earth-dwellers, the Prunellidae feed on insects and other invertebrates, or berries and seeds, which they seek particularly in the soil at the base of thick bushes.

Some species, such as the common alpine accentor, *P. collaris,* prefer to live among the bare rocks of mountainous areas. Nests are built on low bushes or on the ground, sometimes among the rocks; they are always shallow cups made of vegetable fibers and feathers finely woven together. All species are migratory, but those that are mountain dwellers often change altitudes seasonally within a single mountain range.

The lesser gray shrike (left) and the woodchat shrike (above) are members of the family Laniidae. They live in southern and central Europe. Shrikes build a very substantial nest.

The Family Muscicapidae includes many familiar birds, such as nightingales, robins, thrushes, warblers, and many others.

There are nine subfamilies. Almost exclusively, they include species peculiar to the Eastern Hemisphere and Australia and its surrounding area. As far as is known, these birds have spread to the Americas relatively recently.

The Thrushes of the subfamily Turdinae are thought to have spread to the New World more recently than other subfamilies of the family Muscicapidae. This subfamily also includes the nightingales, robins, red-starts, rock thrushes, and certain of the wheatears and warblers. The thrushes are generally medium-sized songbirds with narrow bills. They have the ten primaries, or flight feathers, common to all the Muscicapidae. Many of the approximately 300 species inhabit both North and South America.

The Babblers of the subfamily Timaliinae include about 280 species peculiar to the Eastern Hemisphere. However, they are similar in habits and appearance to the antbirds of the American neotropical zone. As a group they are reminiscent of the warblers and the thrushes, although they do not have the latter's definite migratory habits.

Sometimes the single species of genus *Chamaea*, the wrentit, *C. fasciata*, peculiar to America, is included in this group of energetic, gregarious birds. Some ornithologists place the wrentit in a family of its own, the Chamaeidae.

The Rail-babblers belong to the subfamily Cinclosomatinae. They are limited to Australia, Papua, and the surrounding area. While they are not very well known, members of this subfamily do not seem to be closely related, and certain species bear resemblance to the thrushes and babblers. In

A North American dipper is shown in its natural habitat—sitting on a rock along a mountain stream. In the Old World diggers live from England east across Europe and Asia. In the New World they are restricted to the western mountains of both continents.

general, the rail-babblers have wide tails and small heads, supported by a narrow neck.

The Parrotbills, or Suthoras, of the subfamily Paradoxornithinae are closely related to the babblers, and are occasionally grouped with them. The subfamily contains three genera: *Paradoxornis, Panurus,* and *Conostoma.* The bearded tit, *Panurus biarmicus* of Eurasia, is actually distinguished by black moustache-like stripes rather than a beard. *C. oemodium,* almost a foot long, is the largest of the subfamily Paradoxornithinae.

The parrotbills are distinguished from all other members of the suborder Oscines by their compressed, highly curved bills.

The Gnatcatchers of the subfamily Polioptilinae include 12 species with small bodies and long tails. They are limited to the New World. Gnatcatchers are closely related to the warblers of the subfamily Sylviinae.

The Old World Warblers of the subfamily Sylviinae include among 275 others, such common European species as the whitethroat, the garden warbler, the blackcap, and the goldcrest and firecrest of the genus *Regulus.* This genus also has two North American species, *Regulus satrapa* and *Regulus calendula.*

The Subfamily Malurinae includes the insect-eating Passeriformes native to Australia, New Guinea, and New Zealand. The beautiful fairy wrens belong to this group. There are about 80 species of these Australian wrens or warblers. They are closely related to the Sylviinae, with which they are frequently grouped.

The Flycatchers of the subfamily Pachycephalinae are a group of deviant flycatchers limited to the Australian-Papuan region, Malaya, and the Philippines. These birds do, indeed, have solid bodies and thick heads.

Their calls are pleasant, and the tendency of the males and females of certain species to sing duets has led to the colloquial name "whistlers."

The Titmice and Chickadees belong to the family Paridae. This family has about 65 species that range in length from 3 to 8 inches. They are rather compact in shape, with small, sturdy beaks and typically soft, thick plumage in both graduated and contrasting colors. Some species are predominantly black or white, and a few are crested. The rounded wings are short, while the tail may be very long.

The friendly black-capped chickadee, *Parus atricapillus,* and several other chickadees and titmice of the United States belong to this family.

The Nuthatches of the family Sittidae are small relatives of the chickadees and tree-

The cactus wren is one of the largest and most unusual of all the wrens. It inhabits dry desert lands, making its nests in cactus plants, which predators fear to approach.

creepers. They are called nuthatches because they "hatch," or open nuts with their strong bills. They have the ability to climb the vertical surfaces of rocks and trees, both upward and downward. In North America they are sometimes called "upside-down birds."

Almost all nuthatches live in the forests of Eurasia and North America. The nest is often built in the hollow of a tree or the cleft of a rock, and the entrance is partly closed with mud or clay.

The Treecreepers of the family Certhiidae include five species that range in length from 5 to 7 inches. All are similar in appearance, with long, pointed or rounded wings, and long, graduated tails with rigid quills—similar to the woodpecker's. Their stiff tail feathers assist the treecreepers as they climb trees searching for food. Their diet consists largely of insects, spiders, and small invertebrates. The beaks vary in length but are narrow. Only one species, the brown creeper, *Certhia familiaris*, lives in North America.

The Australian Treecreepers of the family Climacteridae include six species that resemble the Certhiidae but lack the rigid tail quill used for support in climbing.

The Flowerpeckers are members of the family Dicaeidae. The best-known of these 55 species of lively birds is the mistletoe bird, *Dicaeum hirundinaceum*, which hunts insects, sucks nectar, and eats berries. The family is found throughout Asia and the neighboring Pacific islands.

The Sunbirds of the family Nectariniidae often have brilliant, metallic-colored plumage. This family of 106 species is found from Africa and the Middle East to Asia, Australia, and the Pacific islands.

Like the flowerpeckers, the sunbirds gather

nectar and feed on the insects found within the corolla of the flower. Their beak and tongue are specially adapted for gathering this food. Sunbirds are generally small birds with sharp, unmusical voices.

The White-eyes of the family Zosteropidae have a prominent white ring around each eye. They are a homogeneous family of songbirds, and are distributed throughout Africa, Asia, Australia, and the Orient. They are good flyers, and often colonize oceanic islands that are out of reach to most birds.

The Honeyeaters and Sugarbirds belong to the family Meliphagidae. The 167 species of this family are arboreal birds of Australia. The two species of sugarbirds, of the genus *Promerops*, are indigenous to South Africa. However, there is some question as to whether or not they should really be placed in this family.

The honeyeaters have a unique type of brush tongue, well-adapted to sipping nectar. Members of the family vary considerably in appearance and habits. Some species have brightly colored casques and wattles, with folds of skin hanging below the throat.

The Buntings of the family Emberizidae include about 300 species found in North and South America. They are also found in arctic regions. In North America, the buntings are commonly called sparrows or finches. Some 40 species of Old World buntings inhabit many areas of Europe, Asia, and the Orient. Many species are provided with a beak well-suited to crushing seeds, since it includes a growth on the roof of the mouth against which the seeds are broken.

Among the buntings are the cardinals and gros-beaks, whose 12 genera are found only in North and South America. In the United States, these include the well-known car-

The best known species in the family Mimidae is the North American mockingbird (above left). It owes its name to its great talent for imitating the songs of other birds.

The lovely little fairy wren (above right) of Australia is among the most charming birds of that continent. Fairy wrens are Old World warblers, not true wrens. Females are dull, not colorful like this male.

dinal, *Cardinalis cardinalis*, the rose-breasted gros-beak, *Pheucticus ludovicianus*, and the indigo bunting, *Paserina cyanea*.

The Tanagers belong to the family Thraupidae. Most of these 222 species are brightly colored. They are found in North and South America, as well as the West Indies. They prefer forest habitats, where they can live on fruits and insects. Of the four North American species, the best-known are the western tanager, *Piranga ludoviciana*, and the flaming red scarlet tanager, *Piranga olivacea*.

The western tanager is dressed unlike any other American bird. The male is bright yellow with black wings, back, and tail. Its head is red, but in the fall it loses most of the red. The female is a flat green above and yellowish underneath. As one would expect, the easily identifiable scarlet tanager is a bright red, with black wings and tail. This tanager is about 7 inches in length; the female is a bit smaller. Her coloration is a dull olive and yellow.

The Woodwarblers of the family Parulidae are found all throughout the Americas, and are often known as American warblers. Small insect-eaters, some species have dull gray or olive feathers, while others are brightly colored in yellow, red, or orange, with occasional stripes or patches. There are approximately 113 species. Heavy mass migrations are common among the northern species.

Warblers are magnetic attractions for large numbers of bird watchers. More plentiful in the eastern United States than in the West, northern warblers generally winter in the tropics. As they migrate north in the spring—often in large numbers—they can be spotted by alert watchers. On a fine day in May an experienced observer may see as many as 20 species. The warblers' songs, which require study to distinguish, help to identify specific birds.

The Asian paradise flycatcher (right) is a specialized, long-tailed, Old World flycatcher. Small and fragile, it sometimes nests in gardens.

The Hawaiian Honeycreepers are members of the family Drepanididae. The 22 species are distributed only in the Hawaiian Islands. Their varying eating methods have resulted in very differently formed beaks.

The family is an evolutionary textbook since its members have been able to adapt so specifically to many different kinds of food. It is often divided into two groups—the Drepanidinae, whose curved bills are designed for sipping nectar, and the Psittirostriinae, whose short, stout beaks are well-adapted for cracking seeds.

The Vireos of the family Vireonidae include about 40 species. The shrike-vireos and the pepper-shrikes, once considered separate families, are presently classified as subfamilies of the Vireonidae by some taxonomists.

The Pekin robin (left) and the silver-eared mesia (below) are Asian babblers of the genus Leiothrix. Both are prized as cage birds because of their beauty.

The yellow-thighed manakin (bottom) belongs to a South American group noted for its social dancing displays.

All species of this family are native to the American continents. They are often olive green or gray in coloration.

The red-eyed vireo, *Vireo olivaceus*, is one of the most common forest birds in eastern North America.

The American Blackbirds and Orioles belong to the family Icteridae. Some species of this family—which also includes cowbirds, bobolinks, and meadowlarks—construct quite remarkable hanging nests, often up to 6 feet in length. Cowbirds, however, customarily deposit their eggs in the nests of other birds and leave the hatching and rearing to the foster parents. Most of the 95 species of this family are exceptional songbirds.

The best known species in the United States are the brightly colored Baltimore oriole, *Icterus pustulatus*, the more subdued orchard oriole, *I. spurius*, meadowlarks, genus *Sturnella*, and the handsome and very

The king, or golden-breasted, starling (right) inhabits the drier portions of East Africa. This beautiful, long-tailed bird is one of the glossy starlings.

familiar redwinged blackbird, *Agelaius phoeniceus*. The orioles make a finely woven nest that hangs like a bag from a tree branch.

The Finches of the family Fringillidae include 125 species. Among these species are the goldfinch, *Carduelis carduelis*, with its slender, pointed beak; and the hawfinch, *Coccothraustes coccothraustes*, which has well-developed beak muscles capable of cracking the pit of an olive or cherry. The crossbill of the genus *Loxia* features a beak with crisscrossing points that are well-suited for removing the seeds from the cones on pine trees. Bullfinches and linnets are included in the subfamily Carduelinae, with about 120 species. Only three species have been placed in the subfamily Fringillinae.

The Waxbills belong to the family Estrildidae. Many of these 110 species of waxbills are well known because they are favorite cage birds. Natives of the vast regions from Africa to the Philippines, Fiji, and Solomon Islands, most have brightly colored plumage. The fledglings have interesting identifying markings on their palate and tongue.

The Weavers are members of the family Ploceidae. This grain-eating family includes the subfamily Passerinae—the sparrows. Weaverbirds abound in Africa, and there are a few in Asia. Most are highly colonial. As their name implies, the weavers demonstrate great skill in nest-building.

Among the many African weavers are the black weavers, dark weavers, masked

The red-crested cardinal (left) is a South American finch. Like most finches, its beak is well-adapted to crushing seeds, its preferred food.

The red cardinal (below) is found only in North and Central America. Its plumage is bright red; females, however, are brownish, with bright red only on the crest, wings, tail, and bill.

weavers, spectacled weavers, golden weavers, and little weavers. The red-billed quelea, *Quelea quelea,* a member of the weaver subfamily, Ploceinae, is often considered the most destructive bird in the world. Migrating in vast flocks, queleas ravage African crops. They have actually caused local famines.

The true sparrows are related to the weaverbirds. One sparrow, the house, or English, sparrow, was introduced to the United States, where it soon became a pest. This bird, *Passer domesticus,* is now distributed widely throughout the world, in cities and towns and farms. Its length ranges from 5 to 6 inches. The male has a black throat; the female, a whitish one. Although it is a very familiar species, it can easily be confused with native U.S. sparrows.

The Starlings of the family Sturnidae include 112 species, which are found in Eurasia, Africa, and parts of Australia. They range in size from 7 to 17 inches. The common starling, *Sturnus vulgaris*, was introduced to North America, where it has largely replaced the attractive bluebird.

Starlings are versatile songbirds, and some species can imitate the songs of other birds. This is particularly true of the talking mynah bird.

The Old World Orioles are members of the family Oriolidae. There are about 28 species, whose plumage is generally yellow and black. Unlike the American orioles of the family Icteridae, their nest is a simple cup. The Oriolidae are found in Eurasia, Africa and New Guinea.

The Drongos belong to the family Dicruridae. There are 20 species that live in torrid regions in Africa, southern Asia, and the Philippine Islands, eastern Australia, and the Solomon Islands. Possessing a strong hooked beak, they are arrogant and fearless birds, but while they are known to attack larger crows and hawks, they rarely disturb smaller species. Their calls are a mixture of the grating and the melodious. They build saucerlike nests, and generally feed upon nectar and insects.

The Wattlebirds of the family Callaeidae include three species. These are the kokakos, formerly called wattled-crows; the huias, now extinct; and the saddlebacks. In the huias, the bills of the males and females were remarkably different in shape. The kokakos and saddlebacks are found only in New Zealand.

The Wood-swallows of the family Artamidae are stout, insect-eating birds. They are 6 to 8 inches long, with a mixture of gray, black, gray-brown, and white coloring. The wood-swallows are found in India, through much of southeast Asia, Australia, and the Philippines.

The Australian Magpies of the family Cracticidae include ten species that are restricted to Australia, New Guinea, and New Zealand. Bell magpies and butcher-birds are members of this family. They are known for their musical cries.

The Bowerbirds of the family Ptilinorhynchidae include 18 species that are found only in New Guinea and Australia. In most species, the male builds an elaborate bower of twigs and other materials. The surrounding area is then decorated with flowers, berries, lichens, and other bits of brightly colored

material, which are designed to attract the female to the hut. There, in a complex courting ritual, the male tries to persuade the female to mate. The actual nest, however, is separate from the bower and is a simple, concave construction set in a tree. The female is left alone there to incubate her one to three eggs.

The Birds-of-Paradise of the family Paradisaeidae include 40 species. The colors and patterns in the feathers of these birds are perhaps the most beautiful in the world. Black with metallic highlights, or in combinations of velvety shades of brown, red, yellow, blue, green, orange, violet, or white, the plumage is frequently characterized by a series of spectacular feathers springing out in various shapes. Fan-shaped feathers often spread from the back of the neck, flanks, and breast. Crests and wattles decorate certain members of the family.

In the mating season, groups of some species gather at display areas or at the tops of trees, where they perform elaborate courtship dances. Others attract their mates by solo performances.

The Crows, Ravens, Magpies, Jays, and Nutcrackers of the family Corvidae are distributed throughout the world. Among the largest of the Passeriformes, they measure from 7 to 28 inches in length. Coloring is typically black or a combination of black and white, but jays and magpies have brighter touches of blues, greens, yellows, and violets.

Most Corvidae eat all types of food, including insects, fruit, seeds, dead animals, eggs, and small animals. They are bold, active, and intelligent birds. In some respects, no bird learns faster than the common raven, *Corvus corax*. Like parrots, crows can be taught to imitate human speech.

The family Corvidae is sometimes divided into two subfamilies—the Corvinae, which includes ravens, crows, and nutcrackers, and

The hawfinch (opposite page, top) is found across northern Eurasia, including England. Its heavy bill can crack even the hardest seeds, such as cherry pits.

The hill, or talking, myna (opposite page, bottom) lives in India and the surrounding countries. It can imitate the human voice—or a "wolf whistle"—exactly.

The star finch (left) of Australia, a popular cage-bird, is a representative of the waxbills, or grassfinches—tiny seed-eating birds of tropical Africa, Asia, and Australia.

141

This Raggianas bird-of-paradise displays his spectacular plumage. He uses his plumage to attract and court a mate. The plumage of the female, in comparison, is dull-colored. These birds live in the forests of New Guinea.

the Garrulinae, which includes magpies and jays.

The common American crow, *Corvus brachyrhynchos,* is a typical crow. It is a glossy blue-black and almost 20 inches long. They roost at night in large flocks, sometimes with tens of thousands of birds.

The ravens are the largest of the Passeriformes—the common raven is more than 2 feet in length. They are blue-black and have a very large bill. Ravens are found throughout the Northern Hemisphere.

Like the ravens, nutcrackers are also found in the Northern Hemisphere, particularly in evergreen forests. These birds are about 12 inches long. They store their food.

Many persons are surprised when they learn that the often-attractive jays and magpies are closely related to the crows. The familiar American blue jay, *Cyanocitta cristata,* is strikingly dressed in blue, black, and white. Approximately a foot long, it has an erectile crest. It is found in the eastern portions of North America; the American blue jay does not migrate.

Among the jays resident in western North America, Steller's jay, *Cyanocitta stelleri,* is widely distributed—from Alaska southward through most of Central America. Its head and crest, throat, and breast are black; the rest of its body is bluish. It is slightly larger than the blue jay.

The black-billed magpie, *Pica pica,* is found in many parts of the Northern Hemisphere, including the Rocky Mountain region of North America. A black and white bird with a sweeping tail, it ranges in length from about 18 to 21 inches. The yellowbilled magpie, *Pica nuttalli,* is slightly smaller than the black-billed species but otherwise very similar except for the color of the bill. It lives in the valleys of central California. Magpies have a varied diet; they like plant crops and can be a pest to farmers. They construct large, complicated nests of sticks and mud.